D1176536

the

OPPOSITE
of
HIDING

the
OPPOSITE
of
HIDING

How Plant Medicine
Transformed My Life

Shayla Malek

NEW DEGREE PRESS
COPYRIGHT © 2022 SHAYLA MALEK
All rights reserved.

THE OPPOSITE OF HIDING
How Plant Medicine Transformed My Life

ISBN
979-8-88504-631-2   *Paperback*
979-8-88504-949-8   *Kindle Ebook*
979-8-88504-836-1   *Digital Ebook*

This book is dedicated to my father.
To the little boy inside him I've learned to see.
To everything he suffered and all he taught me.

Contents

Disclaimer

———

This book is a personal account of the insights and awarenesses, peace and joy, that I gained from my healing journey using plant medicine. It also talks, however about trauma, depression, suicide and mental health.

If you, or someone you know, are thinking about self-harm and live in the US, call 988 for the Suicide Prevention Lifeline, or text HOME to the Crisis Text Line at 741741. If you are located outside of the United States please call your local emergency line.

This book is not a clinical 'how to' for psychedelic-assisted therapy sessions or a history of plant medicine. I am not a medical or therapeutic practitioner and I am not recommending people try it. While it has been an incredibly valuable tool for me, I know it's not for everybody.

I do recommend though, that if you are interested in psychedelic-assisted therapy, you talk to your own medical professionals and work out if it is an option for you and what support you might need.

Author's Note

Up until the time my father passed away, he was trying to get his story published about him surviving the holocaust. I took on the job, but I couldn't bring myself to do it. I was clearly doing every trick in the book to avoid the task, because, well, in addition to everything else, it's the holocaust. Who wants to sit and think or write about that?

Even though I'd already read it a number of times, it wasn't until shortly before the pandemic, that I finally sat down at my computer to work on editing his book. In it, I knew I wanted to highlight his bravery and tenacity to do everything he could to survive. I wanted to shine a light on his suffering and PTSD along with his survivor's guilt and shame.

I quickly realized that before I could work on his story, I had to first untangle it from mine. While thankfully my story is fundamentally about healing, forgiveness and self-actualization, *our* story is about the repercussions of his ordeal on his psyche, his personality and ultimately, on his actions.

His book ends not long after the war, but I believe his story is not just one of a young boy who escaped the clutches of the Nazis and managed to survive the evil of the holocaust, but is how he dealt with that evil lodged in his heart, and continued to try and thrive anyway. It's how he tried to live a life worth living and build something for his family. It is about how something inside him broke that he never fully recovered from. It was his ongoing struggle with his faith, his hope, and his battle with falling into the depths of despair.

The Hope For Depression Research Foundation website soberly states, "Depression in the US affects over 18 million adults (one in ten) in any given year." And "Is the primary reason why someone dies of suicide about every 12 minutes – over 41,000 people a year."

When I look back at my childhood, now I can see the trauma. I see his unresolved, and mine being acquired. Some was inflicted upon me directly, and some just leached into me from continued exposure to his aura of suffering, which constantly encircled his body like a radioactive corona around the sun.

I'm sure he didn't intend to dump his pain and anguish on me. He didn't mean to teach to my very core that the world is not a safe place. He didn't mean to teach me first-hand that I couldn't trust anyone, or that everyone hates me because I'm a Jew. Or did he? He did however explicitly tell me to hide. Hide my talent, hide my intellect, my strength, my sexuality and femininity, but most of all, to never reveal my religion to strangers. *The. World. Is. Not. Safe.*

So all my life I hid in one form or another. From dangers real and imagined, lurking around every corner. I dimmed my light to keep my world small, and me insignificant, trying not to take a step out of place or attract unwanted attention. I ignored and repressed aspects of my self, believing it was safer that way.

Unfortunately, while hiding may have saved me in extreme circumstances, as a long-term strategy for life, it absolutely failed. Towards the end of 2018 it became clear that

I couldn't hide any longer. I had sunk into my own dark depression and had never before been that sad and scared.

* * *

One of the positive things, however, that I inherited from my Dad was his love of photography. I now have tens of thousands of photos on my computer, and a dozen Ikea wooden boxes on the shelf above my desk, each crammed to the rim with photos and negatives. I display them wherever I can around the house. Snapshots and snap-frozen instances of my life. My partner Joe asked me why I have so many, and why I carted them around. It's simple. I have them because they remind me of who I am and who I was. Without them I would have no proof that there existed a part of me, even if it was only for that instant, who smiled and laughed, played, danced, climbed mountains or otherwise explored the world.

In my darkest moments I would look at those happy photos and wonder who that woman was. Where she had gone. I seemed to have lost any access to the parts of me that were captured in those pixels or celluloid cells. It was as if their vibrancy and opacity had been turned way down to zero on any recent photo of my life.

But then I learned that psychedelics were having a resurgence in the psychotherapy world as a recognized treatment for PTSD, depression and addiction. To the point that in addition to weed (Cannabis) already being legal, in 2021 Seattle voted to decriminalize natural substances, notably psilocybin and ayahuasca.

Researching into the healing potential of plant medicine gave me the confidence I needed to step out of my comfort zone and try ayahuasca, mushrooms and Cannabis to heal my trauma, and I am so grateful that I did.

To be fully transparent and fair, it wasn't only the plant medicine that helped heal me. It was also love and support from those closest to me, and years of a LOT of different therapies finally clicking into place. But it was the biggest booster shot that I ever experienced. It catapulted my emotional growth and healing to places I had never been, and I went there faster than ever before. Plant medicine not only transformed my life, it helped me want to live.

* * *

Mixed in with all the hardships of being the recipient of my father's story, was also my father's one blessing for me as I was growing up. It was "You will always be ok. You will always land on your feet."

I think he was saying that despite the fact he knew firsthand how dangerous the world was, he had made it through, so somehow I would too. He believed that, so I want to believe it too. It was him reaching forward and tapping me on my shoulder with his miracle of survival, passing it on to me.

If I had any children I'd reach forward and tap them on their shoulders to pass on my blessings too, but as I don't, I'm writing down my story to pass it on to whomever needs it. I want this book to be a path of runway-lights of hope, guiding others in similar situations up and out of their own darkness and to a place where self-awareness, acceptance and healing is possible. Because if it was for me, then it might be for them too.

I have no idea whether my father still had his faith in God when he died. For his sake I hope he did. I hope that he had some comfort about going. I hope that he found peace and managed to have a clear soul.

I also hope he knows, I have landed on my feet.

PART 1
Misha/Michelle

CHAPTER 1

There but for the Grace of God, Go I

———

I have three different names I have gone by in my life, neatly delineating my timeline like the rings of a tree. The first, Michelle, was given to me by my parents, and is synonymous with my time growing up in Melbourne's outer suburbs in the 70's and 80's. The second name, Mitch, I donned along with a new personality as soon as I left home, and it helped me feel safe venturing into the world. The last, and so far final name, Shayla, I chose in my late 30s and it commemorates me reclaiming my femininity.

Michelle had fine dark hair, that started straight and then after puberty, mysteriously grew into tight Shirley Temple curls. She had brown eyes and fair skin with a sprinkling of freckles on her heart shaped face. She was the skinny, annoying, persistent younger sister who followed around her older siblings and any of the other neighborhood kids, begging to be allowed to play. Then suddenly she was the awkward teenager, overweight, overwhelmed and shy. She was the nerd and bookworm, who's breasts came in too early, and too large, to not draw unwanted attention and ridicule from the boys at school, or catcalls from men driving by.

I hated being Michelle. I didn't want anything to do with her. She was every memory I wanted to forget and every part of me I wanted to avoid. She represented feeling trapped, powerless, overwhelmed and terrified. She was teased at school and intimidated by Dad at home. All she wanted to do was to hide, and to please, to be the good girl and to stay safe. She just wanted to escape.

But thankfully, that's not all she was. As Michelle, I also had birthday parties and gymnastic classes, trips to the beach and swimming lessons. I had joy, fun, and love growing up; even if most of it was when I was away from the house, or if he was in a bad mood, just away from Dad. All our happiness at home depended on Dad being happy–and our safety too.

* * *

"It's not the trauma olympics. There are no prizes for being the most traumatized." My very wise friend Sumit said to me over coffee one rainy Seattle afternoon. I had told him that I was hesitant to write my story, because I felt it wasn't "bad" enough.

The curious thing about the gift of time and distance, and having healed as much as I have by now, is that I look back on my life and am able to ask "Was I really that hard done by?" and my immediate reaction is to say "No".

I've seen other people who had it way worse than I did when I was growing up. *I lived with one of them.* How did my seemingly insignificant troubles compare to someone who had been hunted, tortured, and then worked and starved, *literally* almost to death? But then I look at my diaries and journals with their pages and pages of vented hurt, frustration and rage. I close my eyes and remember scenes from my childhood, and visceral memories of pure terror come flooding back into my brain.

My dad, Simon, was only 5'9" but he always felt like a giant to me. He was strong, tough and a fighter. When he was young, he even competed as a boxer. He brought into his life as a husband and a father those same traits and attitudes which helped him survive growing up in poverty as a Jew in the early 1930's in rural Romania, in the forced labor camps of the holocaust, and later, as an immigrant in Australia.

"What have you got to complain about? You have it so easy!" my dad would often respond to me, effectively ending any argument, or dismissing any complaint.

It's true. Compared to his life and many others, I did have it easy. I was never kidnapped and enslaved. I never had a broken bone or scars from being beaten, or bruised within an inch of my life. I was never threatened with a gun or a knife. There was always food on the table and clothes on my back. I slept warm in bed every night.

But even though my pain was indiscernible to others, and may have felt minimal to anyone else, it was still toxic and damaging to me. It was a vitriol-tipped drill bit that excavated my sense of self, and eroded my heart and soul. It hollowed me out, and made me the perfect vessel to be filled up with a core of fear, sadness and shame.

This is not my father's story of how he grew up and survived the holocaust. It is my story of how I survived the legacy of heartache and guilt he passed down to me. While my anguish about the holocaust was merely an echo of his, everything about the way he brought us kids up broadcast his suffering and fears, and my siblings and I have had to learn to deal with it in our own ways.

* * *

In July 1997 when I was twenty-six, I had an opportunity to travel to Romania for the first time. As I drove across the border from Hungary I instantly felt like I'd entered a time warp and was viewing the country through my father's eyes.

All my childhood I heard from Dad about Romania. About the food, the people, the countryside, and despite what a miserable time he had growing up there, all the things he missed.

In the distance I saw the craggy Carpathian Mountains of his youth framing the horizon; still with hints of snow on their peaks, with steep and narrow roads winding up through their densely wooded slopes. On the plains below, I passed farmers using scythes and sickles in the verdant fields, and driving horse-drawn carts slowly down unpaved streets. There were handmade, pointy haystacks, piled up in the middle of paddocks carpeted with brightly colored wild-flowers. Chickens and geese roamed free across the pot-holed roads, and so did the sheep.

Even with all the beauty, when I saw the country towns and villages, and how hard it seemed for people to make a living, I understood for the first time what his life was like growing up. I saw and felt the poverty in places that were still barely getting by.

I imagined my father living as a little boy in one of those rustic wooden cottages. Running around with a dirt smudged face and patched hand-me-down clothes, as he dug the soil, planted the seeds and tended the garden. I saw him stopping only to pray quickly with his Grandfather, knowing he had better get all his chores done before his dad came home. I pictured his mother smiling fondly at him as she crossed the yard to put the hand-scrubbed washing on a line in the sun, before returning inside to look after his younger brother and get going with dinner.

The thought that immediately followed was *There but for the Grace of God, go I.*

I am not the slightest bit religious, and barely even believe in God, at least not in the traditional sense, but the phrase felt fitting. My thought was not about the place, but more about the hardships Dad endured, and all he sacrificed to ensure that his children didn't have to grow up the same way he did.

I am so grateful to my Dad that he had the courage to immigrate when he did. I could have been born into a war-torn country under communist rule. Instead I got to grow up in the "Lucky Country" as Australia was called, basking in a capitalist democracy, protected and insulated on the other side of the globe. I didn't have to live and work every day with reminders of unimaginable personal loss, suffering and hardship.

Dad was a hair's breadth close to dying in the Holocaust. There were so many things vying for the opportunity: hyperthermia, starvation, exhaustion, malnutrition, septicemia, and poisonous chemicals, not to mention the constant threat of being shot, beaten, or gassed to death.

Even though he kept thinking and saying he "got off lightly" by *only* being in a forced labor camp and not a concentration camp like the rest of his family, my father talked about his brushes with the biblical Angel of Death (thankfully not Mengele) during the war, and how a miracle saved his life. In truth, there were numerous miracles. Some of those miracles occurred in the form of kind-hearted humans, strokes of good luck and timing, or his ability to blend in; yet, others were in my father's own grit, resourcefulness, quick thinking, and stoic inability to give in to his shadow side. He also attributed it to his faith in God. He believed God saved him.

I believe, in his darkest hour, Dad tuned everything else out and finally listened to his own voice telling him to not give up. His spirit, his inner spark, did not want him to quit. He wasn't ready to tap out at the bottom of his misery pit just yet. He was only twenty-one, and he wanted to live.

For the first few years after the war ended, when some semblance of sanity returned to his world, all he focused on was the relief of being alive and reunited with the remnants of his community and family, and the work of keeping a roof over their heads.

Then, at twenty-five, as a displaced person after the war, Dad left everyone he knew and loved behind, which by that stage was only his devastated mother, his younger brother and a couple of cousins. He jumped at the offer of immigration, in exchange for a two-year contract of paid labor on the railroads in South Australia. He was so desperate to put his nightmares behind him, that he was willing to travel to the other side of the world to find somewhere safer.

"Everyone thought they were in paradise. Those were the golden days." Dad said about his first experience of landing in Port Adelaide in May 1949 and getting to live and work in the Woodside Transit camp. He was safe, he was fed and he even had money to save.

I know how much I emotionally struggled in my twenties, moving to Edinburgh and Amsterdam, and later, in my forties, to Seattle—and most of my family were still alive. They were safe. The people I knew and loved at home were only a phone call or a flight away, while almost all of his were dead; hunted; tortured and systematically killed in the most horrific ways. I don't know how he did it. I feel I only caught a glimpse of the heartbreak and loneliness he endured over the years, his survivor's guilt and shame.

*   *   *

Despite the warm reception when he first arrived in Australia, by the time he moved to Melbourne in 1951, it didn't take long for the shine to wear off, and things didn't quite work out as he had hoped. Rather than leaving his trauma behind in Europe, he brought his unresolved anguish with him. There were a few times before he married my mother, Reneé, when he was heartbroken and completely down on his money, faith and luck. His spark to live had to fight hard to come back, but thankfully, by the time Dad met Mum, in the beginning of 1966, his desire to both live and love, had been renewed somewhat.

"It all happened so fast!" Mum told me about meeting Dad on their first date. At twenty-three, she was the oldest of four siblings but still unwed. She had moved to Melbourne a short while earlier to live with her auntie so she could socialize and meet Jewish men. Her family knew there weren't many opportunities in the small but active community of her hometown on the other side of the country in Perth.

"It was so romantic. I guess it was love at first sight. We were set up by a mutual friend, and he proposed barely two months after our first date. We were married not long after that. The fact that he was twenty years older didn't bother me at all," she said with a smile on her face.

I'm not surprised they fell for each other so quickly. He was smart, handsome, exotic, and charming, and she was slim but curvy, pretty, smart, and shy. Both had matching curly dark hair and brown eyes. I can see from their wedding photos that Mum was happy with the marriage. They both had huge grins across their faces. Her parents, on the other hand, were apparently less than thrilled with the gap in their ages.

From the millions of photos of my sister, Cherie, as a baby less than two years after their wedding, I can see they were both overjoyed to have a child. The hundreds of pictures two years after that with my brother, Maurice, as an infant, tells me they were still in the honeymoon phase.

I'm guessing from just the handful of photos of me when I was born in 1971, that by then the shine had worn off and the realities of raising a young family and starting a business were wearing on the relationship, dimming the sparks on both sides; or maybe, it was because by then Mum realized just how much pain Dad was in. It didn't take long for his frustration and anger to surface, and he often verbally and physically lashed out at whoever was around. I know they were fighting a lot. After I was born, she got depressed and coped by withdrawing, which only angered and frustrated him more. He coped by working all the hours he could. This pattern lasted most of their twenty-seven-year marriage.

Despite the fighting, Mum never stopped defending him. I know they loved each other and us kids too. As an adult, I understand they were trying to do the best they could under the circumstances, but as a child, I had to learn how to keep myself safe, and unfortunately, I learned it the hard way.

CHAPTER 2

Learning to Be the Good Little Girl

My internal chronology tells me I was three or four years old when I first learned I had to be a good girl, but I've been told I was closer to six. It's hard to remember exactly. Most of my memories about my life are hazy, as I was checked out of as much of it as I could be, but this childhood night was one of the times that left a lasting impression. Its intensity emblazoned itself into my conscious memory and forged the keystone of my personality.

While recall of the repercussions are crystal clear, I'm a little fuzzy about the cause or exact events leading up to this episode. I'm pretty sure it was something to do with ruining the cassette and portable tape player I was holding on my lap in the backseat of our late-sixties blue Chrysler Valiant station wagon. I kept fiddling with the buttons and Dad told me to stop, but I didn't stop—at least not until too late. I was inquisitive, tired, and bored. A bad combination for playing with mechanical devices that did not belong to me. I kept pushing the buttons repeatedly in quick succession, and sometimes together until the eventual ensnaring of the tape inside the player's spools and the grating sounds of jammed components drew my father's attention away from driving and focused it instead on me. This was not a good thing.

Back in 1977, we lived in a light industrial suburb of Melbourne, in a small, two-bedroom white weatherboard house backed up against the side of Dad's schmutter factory, where at that time, he made dishcloths and socks. It was late, and we pulled into the driveway after dinner with the extended family. Dad, still seething about the broken tape player, sent me out from the car with a wallop across the back of my head and a warning there would be more to come; however, before he could make good on this threat, I bolted into the house and hid in the back of the old wooden closet in the hallway.

Shortly after, he stood outside it and struck it with his fist, commanding me in his booming authoritarian voice to get out and face what was coming to me. It was inconceivable to him that I would defy him in any way. He had been raised in his family on "tough love" and immediate compliance, and now he demanded that of me.

But I couldn't. I just couldn't do it. I was frozen in place, stuck to the floor of the closet, and hunched as small and tight as I could go—anything to put walls and a door between me and his bellowing outrage.

It was mostly dark in there with small slivers of light leaking through the gaps beneath the door and around the hinges. Jackets brushed against the top of my head, and my nostrils filled with the smell of faded dry cleaning fluid, old mothballs, and wool. I didn't care. Somehow, I'd managed to cram myself in far enough back that he couldn't reach me. It was my safe place.

In retrospect, I'm sure I deserved some level of punishment for what I did to earn his ire. He had given me fair warning, but ignorant of the shortness of his fuse, I had deliberately and naively ignored him. I mistakenly believed that as his little Misha (his pet name for me), I was exempt from punishment. I should have known better but still foolishly poked the tiger and was about to feel just how sharp his claws were.

To my childish sense of time, it felt like an eternity I was in that closet, but it was probably no longer than an hour. Sitting there, my dread mounting every minute, I knew I was only making it worse, but I wanted to put off the inevitable for as long as possible.

It was going to hurt. I knew it was going to hurt. I had seen Cherie and Maurice be on the painful receiving end of that wrath when they disobeyed or angered him for something seemingly way more insignificant. Now that fury was directed at me.

I crouched in the dark and pretended with my eyes shut that I would be okay. Maybe this time he would calm down. He would shrug it off and I'd get away with just being yelled at. Maybe, just maybe, someone would rescue me. I should have known this was a false hope of redemption. I couldn't see Mum, but I could hear her muffled and ineffective intervention. When Dad was like this, there was no calming him down. It was safer to not be around.

At one point, he stopped pounding on the door to swear and yell recriminations at me. "You ruin everything. You are so ungrateful. You don't deserve anything I give you. You have to be taught a lesson about the value of things. You can't just go breaking things that aren't yours. You have to learn there are consequences!" He resumed his pummeling to reinforce his point. "There are *consequences*! Michelle Malek, don't you *dare* ignore me!"

He continued yelling and punctuating his message

with bangs on the door with such intensity I was terrified it wouldn't hold and anxiously waited for the instant it would implode in a volatile cloud of splinters and dust.

I held myself with my thin arms wound tightly around my skinny knees, hands white-knuckled, and rocked back and forth on my heels. I wished I could make myself smaller, or better yet, not even exist. I wanted to disappear. His voice kept rising, his anger feeding on his frustration at my refusal to comply. I could tell he was getting madder and madder as his threats turned darker. "Come out now before I have to get you out! I will tear this whole fucking thing apart. I will go and get a fucking axe and chop it down! Come out here, and I'll show you what happens when you disobey me!" he yelled, slamming his fist against the closet, making it shake.

If it's even possible, I held myself tighter and willed myself to not need to breathe. I wanted to be invisible. To hide. To never be found again. As I rocked back and forth, my thoughts screamed, *Go away! Leave me alone! I'll do whatever I have to do if you will just leave me alone!*

It looped so many times in my head, it etched itself into the chemistry of my body and brain.

As I tell it now, I don't even remember how long I held out in my makeshift fortress, with him alternatively cajoling and threatening me to come out. By this time, Mum had gone to put Maurice and Cherie to bed.

Finally realizing his intimidation tactics weren't working, I eventually heard him say, "Okay. You win. I promise I won't hurt you. Just come out already. You can't stay in there all night. I promise, I won't hurt you."

I didn't quite believe him, but I wanted to. I was so tired and sore sitting like that for so long in the cramped confines of the closet. He seemed to be less angry now and more open to reason. Maybe Mum had managed to convince him to stand down? Maybe he was just tired and wanted to go to bed? Either way, I didn't care. Hope fluttered in my heart at my apparent reprieve. I was going to be okay. He wasn't going to hurt me.

Unfortunately, I was wrong. It was just a false conciliatory negotiation tactic designed to lure me out of hiding. The minute I stepped cautiously out of the closet, he swooped on me and delivered the ultimate betrayal, along with the inevitable belting.

After my father administered the final blow and sent me scurrying off to bed whimpering, I lay there curled up into a tight ball on my side, with tear-soaked cheeks and a raw bottom, trying to process what had happened.

I'm guessing Mum came in to check on me, but I honestly can't remember.

"Are you okay?" my sister whispered in the dark from her bed across the room we shared. But I couldn't answer. Suddenly I found myself in a world I could no longer trust or knew how to navigate.

I didn't know it back then, but I was struggling with my grief at the loss of my previously rock solid and dependable place of comfort and sanctuary in a scary world. Dad had always been who I'd turned to for hugs and cuddles when I was scared—now it was him I was deeply scared of.

*   *   *

There were two lessons I learned after I came out of the closet. The first, clearly, was that I should have stayed there. *The. World. Is. Not. Safe.*

That night, and many times afterward, taught me it wasn't safe to be present and aware and in my body. When I couldn't find a physical sanctuary, I dissociated. Checking out became my go-to strategy whenever I felt verbally or physically intimidated. From then on, whenever I needed a hiding place, I retreated to the closet in my mind.

The second lesson was that it wasn't enough to just be Daddy's little girl anymore—I had to be his *good* little girl and not do anything to get into trouble if I wanted to keep his love. It was a simple equation.

Trouble = pain (physical and/or emotional). Love = safe.

As I grew older, I made the unconscious choice to put into cold storage and hide more and more parts of myself until I became my father's concept of a good little girl. I suppressed my sexuality and my intellect and killed my aspirations. Any part of me that was curious, rebellious, or independent, and especially any part of me that tried to stand up to him, was put to trial against his gold standard and, more often than not, sentenced to archival in ice.

As long as I didn't push it too far, I could have some semblance of what looked like what I wanted. I learned how to negotiate. I learned how to manipulate. I became the model of his good little girl. I hid my power from him and myself and learned how to survive by being compliant.

CHAPTER 3

FTG

I was sitting on the paved portion of our driveway on the section up by the road. It was February in 1985, early evening on a school night, and still light out. The sting of trapped summer heat radiating from the concrete warmed the back of my legs through my thin cotton school uniform, making them slick with sweat. I listened to the incessant buzz of blowflies zipping past my head and swatted one away that tried to sip on the tears rolling down my cheek. I was in trouble *again*.

I had been happily sitting by myself watching an episode of the BBC comedy classic *The Goodies* on TV in the lounge room, waiting for dinner, when my sudden giggling drew Dad's attention. He had walked in from another long day in his workshop a few minutes earlier. His long gray dust jacket was smeared with dark oily handprints, and he sat at the kitchen table behind me, working on a new schematic for a tool making job.

"What's twelve times twenty-four?" he called to me out of the blue, over his shoulder.

Caught completely off guard, my mind went blank and I struggled to find an answer. "Um…" I stalled, looking at him like a deer in headlights, trying to buy time so I could figure it out in my head. But I couldn't. I was frozen. I just couldn't process the numbers. To this day I still can't do mental arithmetic. "You are so stupid!" he spat at me, coming over and accompanying it with a hard whack across the side of my head. "What am I wasting all my money on expensive schools for if you can't even do simple mathematics?" he thundered.

I stood there in shock, trying to process what had happened. I started gulping air and instantly my chest became tight and painful. I knew I should go and get my inhaler, but I didn't want to just yet. Wheezing was my instant get-of-jail-free card whenever I was in trouble with Dad, and I usually milked it for all it was worth.

"Get out of here. Go get your inhaler," he growled as I struggled to breathe and he turned back to his work. Mum was cooking dinner and said something conciliatory but didn't intervene. I wasted no time and bolted out the front door, muttering something about checking the letterbox.

My head was still smarting minutes later as I sat in the balmy evening air in the relative safety of being out of his line of sight. My chest had eased but was still a bit constricted, and I tried to regulate my breathing. I slowly lifted my gaze from studying the line of cartoonishly huge bull ants marching peacefully along the inside of a shaded crack in the hot concrete and turned my eyes toward home.

With a sigh, I realized that night there was no time for play or anywhere to escape. Usually when Dad was on a rampage, I'd go across the road as soon as I could and hide out at my best friend, Christine's, house until it was safe to go home. Even better yet was to be there already so I couldn't be seen to get in trouble in the first place. This time, however, it didn't feel like a wise option. I knew I only had a few more minutes of pretending to check the mail before I had to go back inside and face Dad again.

I had hoped to have more time away so it would be enough for him to calm down. As sharp and sometimes unpredictable as Dad's outbursts were, they usually didn't last after he metered out the punishment. I knew if I gave it a while, I'd be his little Misha again and welcomed with a smile and open arms.

The sun began to set, and magic hour light hung in the air and made the hills behind me glow. The cooling temperatures brought a cacophony of birdsong from the resident magpies, lorikeets, rosellas, and cockatoos, along with the rhythmic white noise of the cicadas. I sighed deeply, wiped my face, and slowly made my way down the driveway.

*　　*　　*

Since I was three years old, we had off-and-on lived on this half acre of barely tamed, rugged, and naturally beautiful bush property. It was a few streets down from the entrance to a national park, forty kilometers away from the center of Melbourne, in the foothills of the Dandenong Ranges. We were in a suburb called Ferntree Gully, or FTG as it is known by the locals. We moved there purportedly to get more fresh air for Mum and Cherie's asthma (mine didn't develop until later), but I think Dad just wanted more affordable land and some space.

When we first arrived, there was little more than pot-hole-filled dirt tracks that passed for roads and not much in the way of other amenities. After a while, Dad bought the house and block next door, and with no fence between the properties, it felt like our yard stretched, unbounded for miles, with tall grass and trees.

As kids, we always roamed free around the neighborhood, disappearing off to go and explore or play as soon as we were released from chores and only reluctantly coming home at dusk when Mum rang the cowbell rigged up by our front door. We were rarely alone. Usually we had each other or another neighborhood child for company for our local walkabouts. Our dogs followed us everywhere and were never on a leash.

On the weekends we often hiked up into the national park or trekked the mile down to the milk bar for lollies and ice creams. Once the road was paved, we skateboarded or roller-skated down the hilly streets and played cricket matches on the one bit of flat road just up from our house. We raced homemade billy carts and bikes with no brakes, off the road and down the steep dirt embankments into our unkempt backyard. Somehow, we managed to skillfully navigate around the huge old pines, native eucalyptus, golden wattle bushes, and the multitude of fruit trees in our path.

The first house we lived in when we moved up was a fairly rundown, small (around 140 square meters), three-bedroom, Victorian style weatherboard. The house had no toilet, so we had to use an outhouse until Mum complained enough that Dad installed one inside. The plan was to live in that almost decrepit house while Dad built a better one down the back of the block. In the end, we only lasted a couple of years in it before we moved to the one beside Dad's factory, closer to town. By the time I was seven, Dad had completed enough of the new house for us to live in, so we relocated back up to Ferntree Gully again.

When I was thirteen or so, with the help from me and my brother as laborers and some local tradesmen to do the things he couldn't, Dad also replaced the old weatherboard house up the front and we moved in a few years later; however, it didn't matter how many times we moved or which house we lived in over the years—our family dynamics stayed the same.

* * *

Living in Ferntree Gully meant that for a couple of years—until I begged my parents to let me go back to the local schools—my siblings and I had a two-hour unaccompanied commute on public transport to go to private religious Jewish schools down in East St.Kilda. Cherie and I went to the girls' and Maurice went to the boys'. Even though we were way out of town, and it was a major inconvenience, Dad still wanted us to know and practice the Jewish religion and wanted us to have what he didn't, which was a good education.

We mostly only kept to the spirit of the orthodox laws and traditions of the religion at home, and even that was only really because of Mum. Dad understood the need to be part of a community and was still Jewish at heart, so even though we didn't have the money for private school, he managed to get us subsidized or scholarships.

I never felt like I fit in with my Jewish classmates when I was growing up. I always felt like an outsider. We didn't come from money, weren't ultra-religious, and weren't even local to the area. I had friends, but they'd rarely want to come over and play.

They'd say, "What? Up there in the sticks? But that's so far away!" whenever the topic of coming to hang out in Ferntree Gully ever came up. I had some friends in my street and at my local schools, but being the only Jewish family in the area, I always felt different there too.

But I didn't mind that family or friends seldom came over. It was a relief. Despite Mum's efforts, our place often looked like a tip. Dad was a hoarder—or at least he would have been if we weren't there to somewhat reign him in. He delighted in nothing more than a trip to the Caribbean Gardens Trash and Treasure Market to see what he could find. He hated to waste and loved repurposing discarded items and having everything he could possibly need on hand. In truth, he also couldn't pass up a bargain. This would have been great, except that he very rarely actually repaired or used what he brought home and it just sat around our house or yard gathering mold or dust. Junk was always all over our property: scraps of metal, bricks, odd bits of wood, plastic piping, old tools, or parts of engines. He also filled up two garages with tools and machines and materials. He filled up the underneath of the two houses too. He just dug further into the foundations when he ran out of room.

He got so angry whenever Mum tried to throw anything away. "You never know when you'll need it one day" was his excuse for all the clutter and mess. The saying still aggravates me and causes friction in my relationship today.

The state of our house made Christine's even more of a sanctuary. It was clean and orderly, her parents were calm and kind, and I could lounge around and listen to music, watch movies, or just play and generally be a kid and somewhat let my guard down. So many of my happy childhood memories were at her house. In the summer we swam in her pool, had dinners of schnitzel with red cabbage and homemade noodles called spätzle, and at Christmas, ate marzipan balls covered in cocoa.

I remember how the first thing Dad did once we arrived in Ferntree Gully was to take us kids across the road and introduce ourselves to the German family living there. Uncle Karl and Aunty Karen, Dad insisted we call them. Christine, their only daughter, a year older than me, became a second sister to me and Cherie.

Looking back, knowing his circumstances, it is so incredible to me that Dad was able to be friends with them, and I am forever grateful he did. He taught me then and there that you can't generalize or hold prejudices. No matter who a person is, there is always common ground.

At the time, I didn't think to question this seemingly inconceivable act of goodwill, but when I asked him about it years later, his response was, "My beef is specifically with the Nazis and not the German people. This family is not to blame for my injustices and injuries."

I think deep down, he missed being understood in a way we couldn't give him and craved some connection to the old country.

* * *

My dad was a mostly self-taught, self-made, renaissance handyman who spoke seven languages and five of them fluently. He spoke with an Irish/Romanian accent because of the man who taught him English when he first arrived in Australia. He worked hard all his life and had survived the hard times because of those skills. They'd made him indispensable and ensured he had food and shelter when he needed it the most. He learned to be a plumber, builder, laborer, photographer, toolmaker, and machinist. First, he'd worked in, then owned, several factories, making everything from tape measures to candles to socks. He could fix almost anything with whatever was lying around in a way that would make MacGyver proud.

I still have clear memories of when I was maybe six or seven, in his first factory where he made socks and tape measures, running around amongst cotton bales and thrusting my fingers into sacks of tiny, brightly colored plastic nibs waiting to be poured into injection molding machines. When I think of my childhood, I still smell the tang of freshly milled wood, the acrid smoke from the lubricating machine oil's friction after a piece of steel was drilled, and see piles of curly and sharp metal filings on the floor.

Dad was creative, inventive, resourceful, and, often, cheap. He worked and saved hard, determined to make a better life for his family—and he never let us forget it.

"Be grateful for what you get. I'm not made of money," he'd say when I tried to complain that I only ever got hand-me-down clothes or something bought secondhand or at the cheapest shops. "You don't know how lucky you are for everything you've got. I never had it so good growing up."

That's not to say he never treated us or bought us things, because he did. We ate out a lot. He wanted to be generous and was when he could. He just wanted to teach us the value of money. He worked hard to pay for my private school education and often met me halfway on a big purchase, like my first car. I still remember a time I was home in Ferntree Gully from university and I left my purse on the table. While I wasn't looking, he grabbed it to take out my money and teach me a lesson not to leave it lying around, but when he saw I didn't have any, he put some in instead. He wanted me to be safe. He wanted me to be prepared. He wanted me to survive the tough times he saw coming ahead.

To that end, Dad made sure he instilled his work ethic in us kids too. Even from the youngest age, maybe six or seven, we all had to earn our keep. After school, and sometimes even on holidays and weekends, we were put to work in his workshops and factories. When I started, I was sorting screws and sweeping floors, and when I was older, I graduated to welding and drilling holes in pipes or assembling products. There was always some task he found for us to do.

It was always "work before play" and hell to pay if we didn't abide by that rule.

Work = contribution = value = love = safe. I learned to amend my original Good Little Girl equation.

One night, when I was around eleven, Dad came in from the workshop, weary and speckled with dust, to find me sitting in the living room, my nose deep in a book. I was always a voracious reader as a kid, and by the time I was nine or ten I discovered my love of science fiction and fantasy and spent as many hours as I could lost in their pages. Mum, who spent as much time as she could escaping into books as well, but especially romance novels, encouraged me by coming home from secondhand bookstores with another Asimov, Heinlein, or Pratchett.

"You're so lazy," he admonished when he realized I was reading for pleasure and not homework. "There's work to be done. What are you wasting your time reading that rubbish for? If you want to read something, read my book!"

Dad's book detailed his experiences surviving the Holocaust. At that stage, it was still only a draft Mum was helping him to write, but he urgently wanted us all to read it, and we did everything we could to avoid it. Over the years, he held that book over our heads like a sharpened guillotine. He tried everything from pleading and guilt trips to threatening disownment from the family. He even had Cherie in tears on the morning of her wedding day. At that stage, she still hadn't read it (all of us kids didn't until a few years after he died), so he refused to walk her down the aisle until he'd made his point and Mum talked him around.

He told me, "You don't know how to love anyone else. You don't care enough about me to learn what I have gone through. You only think about yourself."

As Michelle, I got the message loud and clear. To my list

of crimes, and things about me that were not okay, I added lazy, stupid, selfish, ungrateful, and uncaring.

*　*　*

It is hard for me to reconcile how everything Dad taught me about survival was to hide, yet he was still so desperate to have people read his book. However, knowing what I do about the healing power of telling your story, I regret not giving him that support and relief when he clearly needed it, but as a child, it was beyond me. We learned about the Holocaust at school, and they also took us to the museums and to watch the movies, which on their own were enough to bring it to life for me.

I know you were hurt, sad, lost, and lonely, I wish I could say to him today. *But I couldn't take all that on. I just couldn't. I was a little kid. I needed* you *to be the parent. I needed* you *to take care of me. It was too much. It was just too much grief and anger. Your sadness swamped and overwhelmed me. I couldn't be what you needed me to be.*

I couldn't read your book. I couldn't hear your story. I didn't want to know about the horrific way your family and friends all died, or about the atrocities you survived. If I read your book, it wouldn't be something that happened far away to people I didn't know and love—it would make it real to me.

He needed a therapist. He needed counseling and possibly even access to weed. His anxiety drove my anxiety. His constant stress and fear and his hyper-vigilance of everything I did was too much. It suffocated me. *Literally.* I gave myself asthma when I lived with him. Since he died, I've barely wheezed.

CHAPTER 4

It's a Control Thing

Throughout the years I was known as Michelle, I remained trapped within the sphere of Dad's domain. Since that night in the closet, my world was ruled by his boundaries and desires, not mine. Over the years, I nudged ever so gently with the tip of my toe against that confining balloon skin, testing just how much give it had, and pulling back the instant I hit any resistance.

"You can do anything you want to do, as long as it's what *I* want you to do," was my father's favorite response whenever I pushed that limit too far.

But it didn't stop me from trying. As desperate as he was to keep me contained at home under his judging and ever watchful Sauron's eye, I was equally desperate to escape. By the time I was seventeen, I couldn't bear it any longer. I knew I needed out. So, I buckled up and went in search of Dad to talk about me leaving home and going to university.

Dad was sitting in his office in the house when I walked in to tentatively broach the subject again. The first time I'd tried, it hadn't gone so well. He'd just told me a flat out "no" when I tried to tell him I wanted to go to uni and study English literature.

I can't remember if his office used to be my brother's or sister's room before Mum and Dad repurposed the space. I do remember, though, that his desk was piled high with papers and clutter. His business paperwork was tossed in amongst handwritten draft pages of his book, interspersed with the typed versions my mother had transcribed. Those, too, were now full of scribbled pencil mark-ups and edits in his distinctive style. There were also invoices and bills, equipment catalogs, and checkbooks all messily stacked up on top of each other, some spilling over onto the floor. I remember, because I stared at them instead of looking at him.

"So, Dad, you know how we were talking about me going to uni a few days ago?"

Before letting me finish, he repeated his decision from earlier that week.

"No. I told you already. You are not going to university. It is not good for a woman to be more educated than her husband. You need to learn bookkeeping so you can do the books for your husband's business. Like your mother. You don't need to go to university for that. I can show you how." My father was glowering at me and frustrated I was still raising the matter after he had already passed his decree.

His words were the warning. If I kept pushing, next would come the strike.

My heart thumped wildly, and my fists, jammed into my jeans pockets, curled so tightly my fingernails bit into my palm. I knew better than to speak out against his edict. "But Dad, that's what I wanted to tell you. I got into RMIT TAFE to do secretarial studies. They have a two-year diploma. You said you wanted me to get some practical business skills, right?" TAFE (Technical and Further Education) was vocational. Not dangerous university, with its liberal leanings, arts, English literature, and social studies that could teach me to think for myself and threaten to loosen his vice grip on my mind. I could see his demeanor change at that news, and encouraged, I decided to keep pushing for what I really was after.

"So, Dad, what if I went and stayed at Esther's down in East St. Kilda?" I asked as casually as possible. My cousin was ultra-orthodox religious, and to my dad, that meant I would be more strictly supervised. If I was with family, I'd also be less likely to get up to any funny business than if I was in a flat on my own.

"You know she needs help with the kids," I continued hopefully as I saw him consider the matter. She had four kids under the age of five at that time. "And I already asked her. I can stay on her couch in the living room, and when I'm not at school or studying, I can help her out around the house."

In for a penny, in for a pound, I figured, and I threw in my last bargaining chip.

"It's so much closer than here to get to uni and back. I wouldn't be on the train alone by myself for an hour at night. "It also means I would be closer to my Jewish friends, without you having to drive me to see them all the time," I concluded brightly and stood silent, waiting for his response.

"Hmmm. I'll think about it," he eventually conceded.

He really didn't want me moving out, but he did want me to be safe. In that moment, I knew I had my victory, and as I walked out of his office, I let go of the breath I hadn't realized I had been holding. I knew how much this was going to change the trajectory of my life.

* * *

No matter how old I got, I was still always Daddy's little girl. His "German compensation" baby. In 1970, he found out he was getting reparations money for surviving the Holocaust and, realizing he could afford it, persuaded my reluctant mother, already with two toddlers, to have a third child.

When I talked with Mum years later, she told me she'd had a hard time after I was born. I was a fussy eater who wouldn't latch on, and when I did, I bit her nipples raw. I also had trouble keeping her milk down and threw up constantly. "I didn't know it at the time," she said, "but I probably had postnatal depression."

As a very young child, I always had a healthy respect for Dad as my strict but affectionate daddy and viewed him with childish hero worship and pure adoration. He had always been the one I went to for comfort and solace and often climbed up to snuggle into the safety of his lap. Being wrapped in his muscled arms was my sanctuary, where he provided the parental love and comfort that my depressed mother could not.

But that was the confusing thing. Despite his terrifying patriarchal approach and controlling nature, I knew my father desperately loved me. He loved all of us. He was trying his best. That was what made it so hard to hate him.

When I was maybe ten years old, I saw how terrified he was when I came home limping and dripping with blood after I got bitten just below my left buttock by a neighborhood dog. I saw how pale and clammy he went as he scooped me up and raced me to the hospital and stayed with me for the inevitable tetanus injection and stitches; how freaked out he got whenever I had an asthma attack or any of us in the house was ever sick or injured. I always knew he cared. That was never the problem. He just didn't know how to deal with his pain and grief or control his anger.

He also didn't know how to let me go or how to let me be me.

I understood then, as now, that it came from him losing almost everyone he ever loved. It came from him losing his entire village, friends, hometown, country, language, culture, and, even at times, his faith.

He couldn't bear to lose anyone else. But his soul-paralyzing, intense need for love and companionship went too far. "If you aren't married by the time you're twenty-one, you should come home. And I'll be a husband to you... in every way but the obvious, of course," my father said to me one evening when I was eighteen or nineteen.

Now, years later, I'm sure he meant it with fatherly sincerity that he was just trying to let me know he would always take care of me. If I had failed at trying to find someone by the ripe old spinster age of twenty-one, there would always be a home for me. He would look after me financially. Support me. But at the time, it just sounded creepy. It made my heart sink and my stomach go cold. I felt trapped. Somewhere along the line, his parental nurturing had metastasized into cloying enmeshment.

All my teenage years, he screened my calls from boys and said whatever it took to scare them off, so I never heard from them again. He yelled at me for wearing makeup and called me a slut if I had polish on my nails. I was belted when he caught me kissing a boy and routinely called a whore and a bitch in heat. To him I was guilty of sleeping around and being a flirt long before I'd even lost my virginity. I was shamed for my body and for showing it off. In response, I ate as much as I could to disguise my figure's true shape. Then I was told if I kept eating so much, I would be fat and ugly and no guy would ever want me.

According to him, though, that was a good thing. Because "men are only after one thing and will just use you and leave you."

Forget about socializing with boys or going on dates. I wasn't even allowed to sleep over at friend's places if they had brothers.

The one time, the *only* time, I ever brought a boy home to meet him was when I was twenty and just started dating my first ever boyfriend. We turned up for dinner, and Dad greeted us at the door in his underwear—his oldest, dirtiest, torn underwear. I was beyond humiliated. Beyond embarrassed and ashamed. I was mortified. I hated everything about myself and him from that moment on. I vowed never to introduce him to a boyfriend again. Dad said he did it to test my potential suitor and see how he would react; to see if he would shake Dad's hand and meet his eye. But I didn't care about his reasons, only his actions.

Now, years later, that fury has subsided. I have forgiven him. Now I just see his physical and emotional scars born from complete disempowerment to control the suffering he endured and his need to do anything to avoid more pain.

But back then, I couldn't stand it.

"He told me what to do *all* the time," I recently vented to my friend, Samantha, when we were talking about it one day. "Under his rule, I had to be slim (but not too sexy or attractive), compliant, and loyal." Oh fuck! That was a huge one. I *had* to be loyal. I could only love him. I wasn't allowed to love or be loved by others. Not even by the family. I wasn't allowed to have anyone on my side, no sticking up for me and no talking against him. It had to be about him and his needs. Unfortunately, I don't remember Mum being much help, but that doesn't mean she didn't try. If she advocated for me, it was when I wasn't around, but I'm pretty sure she had a part in convincing Dad to let me move out. She tried to keep the peace the only way she knew how, but just like me, she mostly kept her head down and tried to stay out of his way, choosing when to pick her battles.

By 1987 or maybe it was 1988, I can't remember the exact date, both my siblings had moved out. Cherie had gone as soon as she could at eighteen. She was happily living with friends closer to the city and was now engaged to be married. Somewhere along the line, Maurice had found the religious world of the Yeshiva. He'd gone all in on the religion and even changed to his Hebrew name, Mordechai, which then got shortened to Mordie. When it was time for him to go, he didn't just leave home, he disappeared off to Israel with barely a word of goodbye. Over the years we've sporadically kept in touch but have only seen each other a handful of times.

As tough as Dad was on me, it was nothing compared to Maurice and Cherie. As they were older, they coped with the full force of Dad's discipline. Cherie was a rebel, and Maurice was the only boy, so both had Dad's different expectations thrust upon them. As the youngest, I learned from their mistakes. I saw the things they did which upset or angered him and I made sure not to do the same. As we got older, Cherie and I formed an alliance in coping with Dad and supported each other as best we could, but Maurice was not that interested and preferred to go his own way.

As a teenager, I saw how it broke Dad's heart when my sister and brother left home under less-than-stellar circumstances. As I look back on it now, I understand how bereft and alone he must have felt. How impotent and frustrated that he could not keep the ones he loved close and safe.

When I was sitting down to write this chapter, I went through some old pictures on my computer and found one of him at my twenty-first birthday party. Looking at his face in the photo, I said the things to him in my head I wish I could have had the guts to say when he was alive. *I love you, Dad. I always have. I always will. I just couldn't live with you, or for you. I know you were trying to live through me. You were trying to find those parts of yourself you hid in order to survive. But instead of finding yours, you stole mine. Because of you, I hid those parts away from me, and lost them for a long time. And yet you still taught me a lot of good things and did right by me in many ways. I also have much to be grateful for about the way I was raised. But you resented me equally for it. Everything came at a price; that price was loyalty, my sense of self, and my complete compliance.*

His hyper-controlling wasn't even something I knew was unusual. I thought that was just his style of parenting. I absorbed it unquestioningly, and when his voice stopped, I replaced it in my head with my own.

* * *

I don't remember Dad asking, "What are you doing? Where are you going? What have you got there?" but clearly, he did, because even decades after he died, I found myself asking those same questions in my relationships.

A few months ago, I was home sitting at my computer in my study and was interrupted by my partner, Joe. "You did it again!" he said with his eyes flashing, referring to our previous interaction. Half an hour earlier I'd arrived home from walking the dog and came into the kitchen to find a package on the table. Straight away I'd asked Joe what it was and why it was there when, clearly, I knew the answer.

"All I did was ask what it was!" I immediately shot back.

"But that's not it. It's not just what you say, it's how you say it. Your voice. Your body language. It's a fucking inquisition."

"But it's something that shouldn't be there. I want everything in its place. And when something is out of place, I want to know what it is," I tried to explain.

"But it's not just in the house. You do it in the car, you do it when we are out, and you even do it to other people," he continued, driving the point home.

As soon as Joe said that about other people, he lost me. I was trying to think of the times I did it to him and came up with a few in my head, but as soon as he said I did it to others, I dismissed him as lying. *That's not true at all. Why would I do it to other people? I don't care if their house is a mess. I just care about mine.*

"And another thing," he went on, "when I come home from the supermarket, I can see you craning your neck to see what is in the bag. It's always with my stuff you want to know what's going on. It feels like an intrusion and an invasion, and it's uncomfortable."

He finished talking, but I was no longer listening. I was still churning at the thought that he was a liar. I had to prove myself right. My reaction to his words was instinctive and immediate. I had to defend myself against his false accusations. I would do anything to avoid accepting blame. Blame equaled being in trouble, and the *trouble = pain* tape automatically played.

Unconsciously I immediately became a pilot sitting in a Learjet, psyched up, starting my engines and going through the pre-flight checklist. This time, however, before I took off and engaged him in a verbal dog fight, I stopped and took a breath. *Wait. What if he isn't lying? What if he is telling the truth, and he is observing a behavior I can't and is giving me the opportunity to change it? What if he wasn't trying to just win a power struggle in our relationship? What if he actually had my best interests at heart and loved me and wanted our relationship to work, because he wanted to stick around, and me acting this way was making him miserable?*

Wow!

You mean I don't have to fight him to be me? I don't have to have all my defenses up? I can actually hear something critical about myself and not have to duck for cover? I am safe to admit I was doing something wrong, and maybe, just maybe, I could change it?

Just, wow!

I drew another breath.

What would a calm and present person say right now? What would I want him to say to me if I was trying to tell him this?

"Okay," I said, looking him in the eye. "I'm sorry it is making you uncomfortable. I will make every effort I can to not do it any longer. I know it's going to be hard, because clearly this is subconscious, but I will try my best."

Immediately his stance visibly softened. He had been heard. He had been understood and validated, and the conversation easily moved on to a completely different, neutral topic. The energy in the room also shifted. This was so different from how I used to react. I no longer felt threatened, but my mind was still processing.

"It's a control thing! That's why I try to keep tabs on you in the house, I'm doing to you what Dad did to me!" I exclaimed, as a sigh of dawning awareness rippled through my nervous system, finally letting my whole body relax; releasing decades' worth of tension and expectations of punishment and recrimination. I'd been fighting for so long for permission to be me that I always had my guard up.

"Oh, *I* know! I'm glad *you* recognize it!" retorted Joe.

I just looked at him and smiled. *I was safe. I could relax, let go and just let things be.* For the first time in my life, I truly knew what it felt like to be the one in control of me.

PART 2

Mitch

CHAPTER 5

Dad's Suicide

I have a fourth of September tradition. Every year since 1993, I light a candle and take photos of wherever I happen to be that day and write a letter to my dad in my journal. At least, I used to have that tradition. I think by the early 2000s I was down to just taking photos and lighting a candle. Nowadays I just light the candle.

I was twenty-two when my father killed himself with his old hunting rifle; the one he kept under his bed and I had found many times when I was a kid, nosing around in my parents' personal spaces. It was never loaded, of course, the bullets were never to be seen, and I didn't even know he had any. It was just the rifle, a relic of his past, untouched and gathering dust—until it wasn't. Until he used it that morning, and it sprang back into life so he could end his.

* * *

Since I was eighteen, I had been happily ensconced in a little two-bedroom flat I shared with a succession of flatmates, on the top floor of a two-story apartment building in the middle of Melbourne's Jewish "ghetto" some thirty kilometers from my parents' house. It was a forty-five-minute drive without traffic. The proposed move to my cousin's had only lasted a few months before both of us realized it wasn't going to work, and I moved in with my first flatmate, Ruth, instead. She gave me something I'd never had before: a safe and cheerful home where I was appreciated and free to just be me.

Every time I drove up Burwood Highway, past the Chadstone mall toward the hills and my parents' home, I had the same visceral reaction. With every mile, my carefree, newfound and carefully cultivated positive zest for life ebbed away from my heart, like a slowly deflating air mattress, making room for dread to move in like a boss to reclaim the newly vacated spaces. My dad, like anyone, had his good days and not-so-great days. Unbeknownst to me, by the time I drove up to Ferntree Gully in my occasionally reliable, 1980-something, baby-poo brown Toyota Corolla Coupe to unexpectedly look after him for the week, he had faked most of his good days for the past few months.

I mean, let's be real, I never knew what mood I'd get him in on any given day regardless, but lately it seemed more likely than usual I'd get him when he was feeling particularly cantankerous and down. These were bad days not just for him, but also for any unfortunate who strayed into his vicinity.

I was definitely not looking forward to stepping in at the last minute to keep an eye on him while Mum and Cherie were in Perth for a holiday. It was bad timing, but their trip had already been booked and paid for. An inconvenience, but nothing I couldn't manage. It wasn't the practicalities of the situation which made my stomach drop when Mum asked me to do it—it was the prospect of being the sole focus of Dad's attention for that long.

Dad battled with high cholesterol and angina until he'd had a quadruple bypass operation when I was seventeen. The stint in hospital left him weakened from a golden staph infection, from which he never fully recovered. Then, adding insult to injury to his already struggling attempts to maintain his strict twelve-hour-day work ethic, just after his sixty-ninth birthday, he got diagnosed with the onset of Parkinson's. And now, weeks after he should have been better, he was still recovering from a bout of the flu.

Thankfully, the week was almost over, and miraculously it passed mostly without incident; no sessions where he interrogated me like he was a prosecutor and I was on trial for war crimes, probing for any possible evidence of my inevitable misdeeds. No yelling sessions where he steamrolled over my attempts to direct my own education and life, and thankfully, no talk of me coming home again to stay or the oft-repeated recriminations for moving out—just rehashed conversations about the doomed state of the world and the much-prophesied pending third world war to keep my spirits subdued and in sync with his.

I just had the weekend left to get through, and then Mum would be back on Monday to relieve me. This knowledge lifted my spirits considerably. Friday night dinner passed without a hitch. He was feeling physically much better now the antibiotics had finally begun taking effect. I'd made him a typical Shabbat dinner of chicken schnitzel and salad, and afterward we watched the seven o'clock news in the lounge room, eating our dessert of fruit salad on our laps. It didn't take too long before he started dozing in his chair, his head lolling to the side, his grey hair falling forward and dangling in oiled strands in front of his face.

Later, I roused him from his chair and we got ready for bed. After a few minutes, I popped my head in his door to see if he was in bed yet. He was. I walked over to kiss him goodnight and see if he needed anything.

As I turned to leave, he asked in a tired voice, almost pleading, "Misha, stay?"

He always called me that when he wanted me to be his little girl. "Sleep with me tonight…on top of the covers, of course. You don't have to do anything. Just be here with me."

In that instant, I felt the familiar reinforcement of years of his chiding me for my selfishness manifest as a squishiness inside my stomach and my gut constricted involuntarily at his request. No. I didn't want to sleep beside him. It didn't feel…right. It was the way he asked; not in a sexual way, but it felt off, like he was asking something inappropriate from me and knew it. He had not asked me that since I was a child, when we had to go with him and take a nap, and I was instantly repelled by it.

Willfully ignoring my clenched gut, I took a breath and eventually asked, "Are you okay?"

I was concerned but didn't want to commit.

I waited for the repeated request, but it didn't come. He must have seen my reluctance because he uncharacteristically muttered, "I'm fine. I just wanted some company. I'll be fine, forget about it."

Relieved, I hastily said, "Okay. I'm going to sleep in my room. I'll be just across the hall if you need me for anything, Dad. Just call out and I'll come. Goodnight." I quickly left his room to go brush my teeth.

It was a beautiful spring day that Saturday morning and I woke up encouraged by the thought that I was finally going to get a brief respite and return to normalcy after five straight suffocating days with Dad. As the next day was Father's Day I decided I would find a treat to bring him and see if he would be up for a bit of an outing.

I went in to check on him. I still felt a little weird about his request and my refusal and was relieved to find him awake and bright-eyed with no mention of the previous night.

"How are you this morning, Dad?" I asked as cheerily as I could. "I didn't hear any coughing or sniffing through the night."

"I'm good," he said, smiling. "I'm very good."

"Great!" I said enthusiastically and reminded him about our conversation from earlier in the week. "Okay, so remember we talked about me going to my comedy show tonight if you were better?"

I'd bought the tickets months ago. "And Mum has already organized for Audrey to come in from next door and give you lunch and dinner and to check on you throughout the day."

"Yes, yes. All good," he said, nodding. "I told you I'll be fine. Totally fine. Go."

I continued, "And the show is going to end late, so I'm going to stay at my flat tonight and come back first thing tomorrow. But I'll ring in a few times to check on you."

"Yes, yes. I know. That's fine," his tone was getting impatient. "Go already."

I didn't want to push my luck. I knew how capricious he could be and didn't want to jeopardize my exit route, so I hurriedly left it at that and went to get my things.

In retrospect, it is so blindingly clear he just wanted to get me out of the house; so obvious with hindsight that he had already seen the opportunity of when he would be alone. I don't know when he made up his mind to do it. He had been depressed for so long. So sad, lonely, broken-hearted and angry. And now, so defeated.

I didn't want to see that his failing health was the last

straw added to the pile weighing down his heart. I filtered out the warning signals and missed his true intent.

I left straight after breakfast, eager to put miles between me and my uncomfortable feelings. Every kilometer west I drove toward my flat that day, the more my stomach relaxed and my aura brightened. I was once again moving towards who I wanted to be, rather than who I wanted to escape from. Once I was home, I dropped my bag and phoned my friend, Greg, to confirm our plans to meet at a nearby park. Greg and I sat on a bench in the sunshine, watched the ducks in the pond, and talked about whatever it was that was important to people in their early twenties. I took photos. I felt safe in my own domain again. I felt the delicious, albeit temporary freedom of being unfettered by Dad's bitterness and weighed down by contamination from his depression. But I should have known better.

Nothing good ever came from me being happy. Happy was never allowed to last.

After the park, I hurried home to get ready. By that stage Ruth had moved for work and my new flatmate was not there so I had the place to myself. It was early evening and warm, soft sunlight streamed in my living room window through the newly budded leaves on the trees outside. I think about how blissfully ignorant I was in that moment before the call; before I picked up the handset and my fingers dialed the buttons. How I was successfully masquerading as an average twenty-two-year-old with definite daddy issues, but nothing a few years in therapy couldn't resolve. Then I phoned my dad.

It rang for a long time, until finally a female voice answered. I was confused. Had I dialed the wrong number? It didn't sound like our neighbor. It was only 6:00 pm and she could still be there.

"Hello?" I asked uncertainly. "Who's this?"

"This is the police. Who is this?" The voice echoed back. She probably gave me her name at this point, but I have no idea what it was.

"It's Michelle," I said. "Is my dad there?" Impatience and concern added to my confusion.

"Oh! Michelle. We spoke to your mother. We've been trying to get a hold of you," she finally responded.

I clearly remember thinking that was weird, because there were no messages on my machine and no one had called since I'd been home.

"Where are you? Are you alone?"

"Can I please speak to my dad?" I repeated, ignoring her. "Where is he? Is he there?" I asked more urgently, my voice raising along with the tight thumping in my chest.

"Where are you?" she asked again, more forcefully this time. "I'm home. In my flat," I said shakily as my breathing instinctively registered the impending doom and started to shut down. "What happened?" I asked shrilly. "Is my dad okay? Why can't I speak to him? I want to speak to my father."

"Stay there," she commanded gently. "You live in Caulfield, right? Someone will be over to talk to you soon. Just stay where you are. Are you alone? Is there anyone you can call?"

Even thinking about it now, sitting in my chair as I take my mind back to that day, my torso instinctively starts to rock back and forth. Its muscle memory etched deep, as if with acid. My body's futile attempt at emotional self-regulation.

"I, I, I...my friend. S...s...someone. Is coming. To pick me up," I struggled to get the words out. Thick tears started to clog my throat, making it hard to speak and my legs turned to lead. A horrific premonition crystalized in my brain with a thud at what the realization of her answering the phone could mean.

Recalling it now, I honestly couldn't even tell you which one of my friends eventually came to the door when I failed to meet them at the street for the pre-arranged pick up. Maybe it was Judy or Mark or Tal. I remember the police arrived. Two of them. One a woman. To me now, this scene seems so familiar. I've seen it played out a million times before on TV, but back then, I only had my worst fears that something terrible and important must have happened, but I had no idea what.

They sat me down on the couch and told me...something. I can't remember the words they used to tell me my dad was dead, but I do remember the nausea and sharp pain in my gut when my brain finally processed the news. Everything else about the rest of that night has faded. I'm sure someone stayed with me, put me to bed, and maybe tried unsuccessfully to get me to eat. It's all a blur—I was clearly checked out. All I remember was my stomach churning at the self-recriminatory thoughts crystalizing like jagged shards of solid poison in my heart.

He's dead. I left him. I left him and now he's dead, I thought over and over again.

And it's my fault.

* * *

I couldn't have survived my childhood without my friends, and Dad's death couldn't have made this more true. Mum and Cherie were on the other side of the country and couldn't get a flight back for a few days. I was in shock, and beside myself with denial and grief. I cycled through being confused and hurt, ashamed, scared, sad, and angry.

My recollection of the next day and those that followed are still hazy. I guess even today, my mind is trying to protect me.

I remember my close friends (I couldn't tell you who) drove me up to Ferntree Gully to talk to the police and stayed with me through the ordeal.

I had to go to the police station, where they questioned me further about his state of mind. They asked if he had made any threats or previous attempts, and told me the neighbor who found him was shaken, but fine.

That night I went to my friend Tal's place, and I owe his family a debt of gratitude. His mother, Rachel, took care of me. She made me a warm bath, tried to feed me, and let me cry. She consoled me and put me to bed, where we both knew I wasn't going to get any sleep. Without her nurturing comfort when I needed it the most, I honestly don't know how I would have coped.

Mum and Cherie returned as soon as they could on the Monday. They were equally in shock and denial, but we supported each other. I don't remember them blaming me in any way, but that didn't matter. It wasn't *their* forgiveness I was after. My friends and family rallied close by. I drew on their strength, love and support to get first through the funeral and then the emotional aftermath. I don't remember how long it took for the initial shock to wear off and for my anger to surface as indignation at what I was sure was Dad's betrayal. I was so pissed off at what I felt was his abandonment, that I used it for years to mask my guilt, shame, and sadness. "I tried to be the good girl," I'd say to anyone who would listen, whenever the topic came up.

"And for what? In the end he fucking checked out anyway. Left me alone and stranded. I did everything 'right', and the one time I said no, and did something for me, he taught me the ultimate lesson. Brought me straight back into line. Killing yourself on someone's watch was the ultimate power move of spite."

I don't know how long I held on to that anger until my empathy for him made me realize he probably had simply had enough. I had initially only seen it from my own world view, when it most likely had nothing to do with any of us.

I still think about what would have happened if I had stayed, or even if I had honored his request and slept beside him the night before. Could I have prevented it? Maybe. I have no way of knowing for sure, but I think it wouldn't have made a difference. I know he was suffering. He was clearly done and I believe he didn't want to be a burden on us, or to have to live the rest of his life as an invalid. This time, his spark to live wasn't strong enough.

At the time, the implications didn't even occur to me of what his failing health and not being able to work any longer would mean to him. How his experiences in life and in the forced labor camps had ingrained into him that *work=productive=valuable=safe.*

I think he wanted what he had been fighting for his whole life: a dignified death on his own terms.

But back then, before I had those insights and forgiven myself for him dying alone and his story unwitnessed, I don't know which repercussion cut deeper: the shame of being a bad daughter, selfish, uncaring, and disloyal (guilty as charged), or the fear of losing anyone else without even a chance to tell them I love them or to say goodbye. Either way, the shame and fear stopped me from getting into a relationship for at least a decade.

While Dad's death gave me the opportunity over the

years to breathe and let my incarcerated parts come out of hiding, the guilt at feeling relief at how his demise brought about that early release, was something that never really went away.

CHAPTER 6

So, How Do You Feel?

At the time of my father's death, I was in my last year of university and working casually at a recruitment agency rewriting candidate résumés. To say I wasn't coping was an understatement. I remember sitting at my desk staring into space, my eyes tearing up uncontrollably and without warning. Anything would set me off. I was distant and withdrawn and uncharacteristically quiet.

I don't remember how long this went on before my manager, Steven, and the CEO of the company, his brother Alan, sat me down.

"You need help. There's no shame in it. You've been through a tragedy and something quite traumatic, and I recommend you get some therapy," Alan said gently.

"I know of an excellent program I highly recommend. It's a week-long residential and personal growth retreat held in Byron Bay and does deep transformational work. It's called the Hoffman Process. If you are interested, I'd like to gift the cost to you."

Those words were such an incredible act of kindness and generosity from someone who was neither family nor a friend and didn't have any contractual obligation to provide me that level of support. He was a true leader who could see that one of his staff was struggling, and rather than being punitive for poor performance, he paid for me to get the help I needed.

The Hoffman Process, according to its website still today, "helps participants identify negative behaviors, moods, and ways of thinking that developed unconsciously and were conditioned in childhood." And I can say that is definitively true. It opened my eyes along with my heart. It taught me about patterns of behavior and how what you think affects your physical, emotional, spiritual, and intellectual aspects of self. Never before had I felt safe going to anyone professional for emotional guidance. For some reason, Dad was dead-set against counseling or therapy. I never believed I was allowed to have anyone be there to just listen to me, and first I had to overcome a lifetime of training of not airing my dirty laundry.

I used to hate it when people would ask, "How do you feel?" because I just didn't know. I didn't have access to my somatic or psychological feelings. I was so dissociated and out-of-touch with myself. My emotions were trapped behind a sheet of shatter-proof ice—inaccessible and distant.

It was a revelation finding out about myself that way. For the first time, I got a tour of the prison I'd created inside of myself. In my mind's eye, I saw raised up high, in rows stretching far and wide, what looked like two-dimensional Barbie boxes, stacked one on top of the other and side by side. Each contained a snap frozen part of me, flattened between two sheets of ice: trapped specimens on microscope slides. They were the parts of me I'd sentenced to archival on ice when Dad found me guilty of doing something he didn't like. Each of those cells were dark and still, my incarcerated parts deep in cryostasis, and cut off from the rest of my personality.

When I came back from the Hoffman Process, I was like a new woman. I'd managed to break through my initial defenses and get a lot of those parts back out on parole. I had access again, even if it was limited, and sometimes only temporarily, to my creativity, drive, sense of adventure, and determination to live my life.

I now had the vocabulary and understanding of what I had done when I put my parts into a deep freeze to cope with Dad. I finally understood it wasn't the real me that was numb and constantly dissociated, but just my response to a lifetime of distress. It gave me hope and the support I needed to thaw those parts out and let them, and me, breathe.

The biggest gift from the Hoffman Process, however, was it gave me, for the first time in my life, someone I could talk to as the real me: scared, sad, and lonely. Someone who spoke my therapy language.

It was where I met my very dear friend, Alison. She had just lost her brother to suicide and we bonded over our feelings of loss and our desire for healing. "They don't really understand," I'd lament to Ali, knowing she would.

At twenty-two, most of my friends still had both their parents or hadn't experienced this level of trauma. She was the one I'd call at midnight when I was overcome with grief and we processed it together.

* * *

By the time my father died, my second name, Mitch, had already been thrust unceremoniously upon me a few years earlier. I was eighteen and had just started my first year of university.

I was doing the regular lunchtime pub routine with my classmates. At one of those liquid lunches, my very good (and possibly also quite drunk) newfound friend, Simone, tried to say "Michelle" and it came out as "Mitchell." Almost immediately, Mitchell became Mitch and stuck for two decades.

Mitch was as far away from Michelle as I could be.

Whenever anyone innocently committed the seemingly heinous crime of calling me by my birth name, I'd correct them vehemently. "It's MiTch, not Michelle or Mish or Misha," I'd say, strongly emphasizing the T.

That one letter was my sole claim to my own sense of identity. With the added bonus, of course, that Dad hated it.

"It's so butch," he'd complain. "Why do you have to choose a man's name? Do you want to attract women? You have a perfectly good name already. Why do you have to go change it?" he would ask, annoyed, whenever he heard it.

But I deterred, and the name stuck; at least, outside of the family.

I loved being Mitch. Over the years as Mitch, I became brave, adventurous, curious, flirtatious, sexually active, university educated, and, best of all, an independent world traveler. I no longer lived in the socially isolated outer suburbs with my overbearing father and moved between the hipper, vibrant, inner-city Melbourne suburbs of East St. Kilda, Port Melbourne, Armadale, East Malvern, Rippon Lea, and Windsor. I had a vast, eclectic, and busy social life, with friends of all faiths and persuasions, collected from workplaces, studies, and various activities.

I played indoor beach volleyball, ran—okay, more like jogged, walked, ran, and then hobbled most of—a half marathon and other races. I hiked up mountains and went skinny dipping in lakes, did triathlons and cycled 210 kilometers in a day (twice) for charity. For a little while, I even wrote a column in a cycling magazine.

I worked in tech and studied photography. When I was twenty-four, I went overseas for the first time, where I lived and worked in Edinburgh and later in Amsterdam. I traveled all over the world. There was nothing I couldn't do and nothing I couldn't be. As Mitch, I was free.

At least, that's what I told myself when I was her. I pretended like I had everything under control. I fooled a lot of people, including myself, that I had my shit together, but I didn't. No matter how much therapy I did, and I did *a lot* during my time as Mitch, I still had a well of deep, unresolved grief, fear, and pain inside me. It constantly lurked just under the surface, threatening to leak out at any moment and drown me, and anyone nearby, in an unchecked emotional tsunami.

* * *

Unfortunately, in just one week of the Hoffman Process, I couldn't get to all my core issues. It was just the start, and I had so much more work to do. By 1997, toward the end of my time in Edinburgh, I was struggling again. I tried to be positive and happy, but it was taking every effort to keep my negativity buried, and often I retreated to my room in tears. I was living with my friend, Doug, who I'd met at ballroom dancing, in his tiny, two-bedroom walk-up flat in Polwarth when I discovered Co-counseling.

The therapist I was seeing at the time recommended it to me. "It's not for everyone," he said. "More like the 'worried well,' so not people with psychosis or who can't hold attention and space for themselves or others. It's not a replacement for therapy, but a safe space to explore your feelings in more of a peer-support network setting, where you swap between being the 'counselor' and being the 'client,' so everyone is equal. You have a great capacity for emotional analysis and high levels of empathy, so I think it would be perfect for you."

I'd seen a few therapists since the Hoffman Process, but it was expensive and I didn't have that kind of cash to burn. He told me that to qualify to join the Co-counseling community, first I'd need to pay to do a forty-hour training course where I'd learn the skills and theory but would also be assessed on whether Co-counseling was right for me. After that, the only thing I'd exchange was equal time and energy with any other qualified co-counselors who agreed to do a session with me.

I jumped at it and have never looked back.

CCI (Co-Counseling International), or Co-Co, as we shorten it amongst ourselves, was a missing piece of the puzzle. It reinforced all the theory the Hoffman Process outlined but gave me more tools and techniques to dive further into my psyche. It reiterated that we all have an innate ability to heal ourselves given the right circumstances. It also gave me what I had so desperately been missing: role models and a community.

The Co-Co community helped me truly be Mitch. If it wasn't for Co-Co when I went overseas, I would have immediately regressed back into Michelle. They taught me about an intentional culture of validation, something I had never really experienced before. They highlighted the positive and lifted people up instead of tearing them down. It gave me a space to feel safe, which was such an incredible gift. It allowed me to re-emerge like I'd never done before, and I discovered parts of myself for the very first time.

I was reflecting on how much I had gained from doing Co-Co with Cherie one evening over Zoom. " I can't begin to thank them enough. I know rules are often broken, even within a well-trained and intentional community, but at least they have them. They genuinely try to walk their walk. I have never, in any single interaction with any co-counselor, been yelled at, belittled, or threatened. That's more than I can say for the house we grew up in!"

* * *

CCI started in the USA back in the '70s. Dency and Tom Sargent, along with John Heron, broke off from Re-Evaluation Counseling (RC) and started CCI. I was honored to get to know Dency, her daughter, Cathy, and a lot of the other gifted teachers and practitioners internationally.

"Ok, Cathy, how would you sum up Co-Co?" I asked her when I knew I was going to write this chapter, and wanted a precise definition.

"The practice of Co-Co braids cognitive, behavioral, and emotive therapeutic techniques with an emphasis on emotional intelligence and strength-building," she responded almost immediately. As a therapist and Co-Co teacher she is used to describing it formally.

To put it more simply, it means it taught me techniques from all types of therapeutic backgrounds and modalities. It taught me how to change not just my behavior but also my thoughts and to learn to recognize and name my feelings. It also taught me how to be more emotionally resilient; exactly all the things that Brené Brown talks about in her books about vulnerability and having an emotional vocabulary.

I love the principles of CCI: that of confidentiality, non-judgment, and the "client" (the person working) is always in charge. It meant I had full control over my session when I was doing my work and the other person or "counselor" was there, giving me their dedicated attention, keeping me safe, and if I wanted, helping me, through probing questions, to dive deeper.

When we first met and I was telling Joe about CCI, I tried to explain why, decades later, I keep giving it my time and energy. "It's more than just a place I found to process my emotions. All over the world, wherever I went, I found safe havens and safe homes within the CCI community. So many people hosted me for workshops sight unseen, inviting me into their houses and lives. I found a family of choice when I needed it the most. I felt wanted, cherished, and loved when I was so far away from my family and friends back home. In so many ways, it saved me."

Even though I've been to a ton of international workshops over the years in Hungary, New Zealand, and the Netherlands, it was at my first CCI-USA workshop in '98 where I fell in love with their community in particular. As there was no CCI in Australia at the time, I adopted it as my home base, and they welcomed me with open arms. Northampton and Hartford became my new regular destinations, and I went back every few years, to do workshops and hang out. There I found more close friends like Ali, where I safely shared the most vulnerable parts of me.

"But that's not all," I continued telling Joe, "The most valuable things Co-Co gave me were the skills, tools, and knowledge to be a better therapy client."

With their help I practiced over the years how to go into observer mode, where I could gain a more objective view of my own behavior and see my patterns—the ways I got stuck doing the same thing over again even though it no longer served me. I learned how to release emotions physically through catharsis (like yawning, shaking, or tears) and how to be okay to let them ebb and flow. I learned to not be afraid of ugly crying, wailing tears, and snot, whether mine or anyone else's. It also gave me the crucial steps of analysis and re-integration to help me figure out what came after the tears and insights.

Another gift it gave me was exposure to many different healing practices. The CCI workshops are all co-created, facilitated, and run by community volunteers. We all contribute to the content of the sessions, based on what we would like to offer or receive. Along with standard format Co-counseling, I did sessions on practices including alternative therapies that worked with the body instead of the mind, like re-birthing, emotional freedom technique (EFT), craniosacral, rolfing, and bowen therapies.

It lit the fuse for self-discovery, and as Mitch over the years, I tried everything from energy work like reike and kinesiology to hypnotherapy and crystals; anything to help me discover my true self and break the tether I still had to my dad.

Thanks mostly to Co-Co, over the years I broke more and more parts of me out of jail and let them run free. As Mitch, I wandered all over the world, doing all the things I never thought I'd do if Dad were still alive, and I was still bound, trapped, scared, and guilt-ridden to his side.

However, therapy wasn't a panacea, and in some ways, I'd still only scratched the surface of all my emotional issues. I still hadn't gotten to the core of my sadness, pain, and grief. I was still running away and using the tactic of keeping busy and active to hide and distract. I didn't want to open Pandora's box. I feared what I would find deep inside—and that I could never put it back.

* * *

As much as I loved being called Mitch, and the air of bravado and tomboyishness it gave me, by the time I was thirty-nine, I'd had a few month-long relationships and only one that had lasted barely longer than a year. I was sick of being single and was ready for what came next. I knew I'd been suppressing the part of me who wanted a family and a life partner; who wanted to be an independent woman and separate identity from my father; the part of me who got in trouble for attracting men. It meant trying to embrace my sexuality and feminine side, and with it, a complete rebranding and time for name number three.

One warm, rainy night at the end of 2009, I was at an alternative lifestyle bush-campout festival in rural New South Wales called Confest. This was where, when I was back home in Australia, I found an intentional community of people with a mindset of tolerance and safe exploration, similar to those in CCI.

I sat on dust-covered rugs in the communal marketplace tent with a few friends, some alcohol, and people singing and playing the guitar in the background. We workshopped a few options before I realized "Shayla" was the right name for me. I loved the way it sounded on my tongue. Every time I said it, I swung my hips and emphasized the final "'la." It conjured up the image of me being a curvy, sexy belly dancer with jingly veils and smoldering dark eyes, confident in my ability to attract any man in the room; everything I aspired to, but was afraid to be.

Shayla is going to be the best damn version of me, I promised myself as I took on that moniker and desired identity.

PART 3

Shayla—The Before Times

CHAPTER 7

Fuck Cancer!

———

It's amazing how hard it was for some people when I told them my new name. Maybe they felt uncomfortable about me stepping out of the "Mitch" box they had me in, or maybe some people are just slow to change and are set in their ways; either way, I didn't care. I didn't need their permission. I shed my skin, and it was time to grow again.

My first few years of living as Shayla in Melbourne were as good as the Mitch years had been. My calendar was littered with entries like: 4:00 p.m., *pole dancing with Deb and Tanya*; 11:00 a.m., *laugh yoga at Fawkner Park*; 12:00 p.m., *Five Rhythms Dancing at Abbotsford Convent*. I traveled, went to CCI workshops, and went on dates. I did my hair, wore sexy outfits and makeup. I even got into a long-distance relationship.

I spent all my time outside of work socializing with friends. I had dinners out, photo sessions, and pub nights, went to housewarmings, themed dress-up parties, and Christmas fundraiser pub crawls. I had standing dinner and walk plans with my closest friends and monthly girls' nights. There were regular open mic events with the Jewish Confest crowd and catch-ups at the Espy Hotel with my friends from uni, with its beer-soaked carpet and views of the sun setting over the beach. I went on camping trips, saw reruns of classics at art deco theaters, and enjoyed work drinks.

However, as much as I wish I could tell you that the Shayla era of my life has been all smooth-sailing and nothing but happiness and glee, I would be lying. I wanted to divest myself of being Michelle and move on from being Mitch, but they, and all their issues, came with me.

One afternoon in September of 2011, Mum called me. "It's stage four. It's in my pancreas and has metastasized to my liver," she stated matter-of-factly. "I didn't even know anything was wrong. I thought it was gallstones. They found it when they did the ultrasound. I start chemo in a few weeks."

This was my first experience of anyone I knew and loved getting cancer. I know my immediate reaction when I heard the news should have been my concern for my mum and what she was about to endure, but truthfully, it wasn't.

I should have known! was my first thought.

At least it's not my fault, was my second.

I wasn't as close to Mum as I was to my dad growing up. When I was little, my dad was my hero. Ironically, when Dad was in a good mood, he was my safe place from the world and where I felt the most protected. Mum was rarely around, and when she was, it felt like she barely wanted anything to do with me.

What I remember about Mum back then was she was always more reserved than Dad and kept a lot to herself. My aunty recently told me Mum was the same when she was a child. She often preferred reading, doing tapestry or embroidery, crossword puzzles, and playing card or computer games to hanging out with the family. As we grew older, she expressed her love through food and took us shopping, finding some tasty treats for us to eat. She always took care of our health and our needs, like schlepping me around to doctors for my asthma and to allergy specialists. When I was in uni, when she could, Mum also gave me money or bought my groceries when I needed it. My fondest memory of Mum when I was growing up was listening to the BBC version of the *Hitchhiker's Guide to the Galaxy* on the radio when she drove me around. When I was older, we went to musicals together, and at home I'd hear her humming tunelessly to classical music.

The closest I've ever felt to her was back in 1999 when I was living in Amsterdam and she came to visit. I saw a completely different side to her from the woman I knew as a child. I saw a curious, open, fun, and engaging woman. I saw the parts of her she had clearly put on ice to cope with living in her marriage.

In truth, it was in the years after Dad died, when she was living with her sister, Hilary, back in her hometown of Perth, that she was the happiest and most relaxed I'd ever seen her. That was when I think she fully came alive, also freed from being by Dad's side. Even though I was on the other side of the world (or country) by that time, we grew closer than when I was a child. Her deterioration was hard to see, and it really upset me. Thankfully her downward slide wasn't initially as far or as fast as I had feared. Mum's rounds of treatments worked all the way through 2012 and kept her mostly in good spirits and fair health, and that helped me ignore the looming eventuality.

I traveled to Perth as often as work would allow and visited and helped out where I could, but I wasn't needed. Hilary had worked in an oncology department, so she knew the routine, and Cherie, who was studying nursing at the time, effectively sorted out Mum's care between them.

* * *

When Joe and I first started interacting online at the beginning of February in 2013, it was in an invite-only
photo-sharing and discussion community. I was home in
Melbourne, and he was in Philadelphia. I was house-hunting
to buy my own place and had just bought, for the first time in
my life, a brand-new car. I wasn't looking for a relationship
and definitely not another long distance one. My previous
one of two years, had ended badly six months earlier, and it
took me a long time to recover.

A few days after Joe's and my first video chat, I told my
friend, Annika, the gossip. "I don't know, there's just something
about him," I said between breaths as we jogged along on our
training run for our first ever obstacle course race that March.

"He's so easy to talk to. We have the best conversations,
even over email. He knows shit about everything!" I laughed.
"Music, politics, pop culture, sports, movies. You know, all
the stuff I know absolutely nothing about!" I gushed, clearly
smitten.

I continued gushing, this time to my friend, Anna, the
next time we had dinner. "We bonded over *Game of Thrones*
of all things! Oh, and photography. I love that beneath that
super cool exterior he's such a nerd!"

"He's clearly making you happy and has great taste," she
observed. "I can't wait to meet him!"

"I'm not going to lie," I told my friend, Suzette, over
avocado Vegemite toast at brunch one Sunday morning a
few weeks later. We'd just walked along the beach path and
stopped for a well-earned refueling break. "We're so different
in so many ways, apart from the obvious him being Black
and me being white, but he seems to get me in a way no other
guy has before."

I had no idea how cute he was until he sent me that first picture. I was blown away. A huge, self-effacing yet cheeky grin across his face, lighting up his deep brown eyes. I knew he was younger than me at thirty-four (I was forty-one at the time), but he had an old soul and felt wise beyond his years. I sent him photos of me framed so they captured my best side. "I need this," I told my friend Donna, referring to my relationship with Joe. She was driving me home one March afternoon from the airport after a trip to see Mum. "This shit is hard to do alone."

"But you aren't alone. You have us," she replied. "Yes! Thank you!" I said, crying.

I felt from the start that Joe was out of my league but chose to ignore it. I needed to feel wanted, appreciated, and desired. I needed to be wooed.

So, wooed I was. I let myself get so caught up in the romance and the excitement of the new relationship that I barely let myself acknowledge the signs that Mum was losing her battle. She'd had enough of chemo and all the side effects and was exhausted all the time with no appetite.

By the end of that April, her spark dimmed to the tiniest of flickers, and she gave up the fight. Hilary and Cherie did most of the heavy lifting of her day-to-day needs, but by then, they also organized a home-visit nurse for pain management and end-of-life care who prescribed Mum morphine. After that, she was rarely lucid.

They let me know she didn't have long left, so I flew over as soon as I could. I got a shock when I saw her. She had wasted away to a husk of her former self. Her paper-thin skin sagged off her emaciated frame like the Holocaust survivors of Dad's nightmares. She lay on the bed in her cotton nighty, curled into the fetal position, and moaned softly in her sleep. It hurt her to be touched, so I just sat by the bed and watched her breathe.

When eventually she passed, I was the one who found her. I came into her room, and my heart jumped instinctively.

I listened hard for the sound of her breathing. I couldn't see any movement, and I knew she was gone. I called out to Cherie and Hilary, and they came in to attend to her body. I couldn't touch her. I was repelled backward. It was the first (and only) time I've ever seen a dead body. I was freaked out and unable to function.

Later, when I videoed with Joe to tell him the news, I voiced how glad I was that he was there for me.

"Thank you," I said with heartfelt appreciation, wiping my eyes. "Through all of this, I needed a rock, and you have been the rockiest. You've helped keep me sane by giving me a much-needed distraction and shoulder to cry on. Even if it is just a virtual, long-distance one."

After Mum died, I threw myself into our relationship. I couldn't wait to meet him in person. I didn't realize how tall he was until his full six-foot frame was bending down to kiss me at our first meeting at Melbourne airport at the end of May. It was amazing seeing him in 3D, and I loved his deep voice and the dark brown tones of his skin.

After that short visit, it cemented what we both already knew. This was real. We wanted to be together, but the problems were where and how. After he left, I suddenly realized how few Black people there were in my life or city. "I'd feel like a pepper corn in a salt shaker," Joe remarked when the subject of him moving to Melbourne came up. Every part of me instinctively understood the need to fit in, so we focused on me moving to the US instead.

Even though we were in love, we barely knew each other. We had only been dating online for a few months when I accepted the job offer from a major tech company in Seattle and decided to leave my well-established life behind to move to the other side of the world. It was destiny. It simultaneously solved the relocation and visa issues and ended the US or Australia quandary once and for all.

"It's a calculated risk," I said happily, as much to myself as to my friend, Shelley, who questioned the move. "I can come home if it doesn't work out. It's not as if I don't know anyone. There are at least a couple of people there I've met before. And I have my Co-Co friends on the East Coast if it all gets too hard. Oh, and don't forget about Skype! We can video any time."

To be fair, when I agreed to move in with Joe, I now recognize that as Shayla, just like when I was Mitch, I was in equal parts running away as I was running toward. It wasn't just the recent death of my mother I was escaping, but also the strong pull of needing to be with someone who helped me feel young and alive. I said yes to moving to Seattle and didn't think about the situation I'd be landing him, or me, in.

CHAPTER 8

Welcome to Seattle

———

Somehow, I had forgotten how to breathe. I exhaled and then forgot to inhale. Mouth agape, lungs still, my carbon dioxide levels sending the emergency dials into the red; then, with a sudden sharp intake of air, I raggedly drew in more oxygen, and the cycle started again.

I was sitting doubled over on the stoop of a house a few doors down from a busy Italian restaurant in a popular part of Seattle. My mouth was slack-jawed, my throat dry as if I'd swallowed 100-grit sandpaper and unable to support it any longer, my head hung low, swaying between my knees.

Joe sat beside me. He was more confused than concerned. "Shayla, you're going to be fine," he said reassuringly, registering the panic in my eyes. "Just sit up and breathe."

I noticed he wasn't making a huge deal about the fact that I'd seemingly lost all connection with my autonomic functions. A part of me was relieved that he wasn't reacting like I was about to die. The other parts of me, however, were *convinced* I was about to die.

My heartbeat was an out-of-sync, defective metronome pounding in my chest, skipping and jumping erratically. My lungs were on fire, and the roiling in my stomach rivaled any supervillain's bubbling vat of acid.

It seemed that along with my natural ability to effortlessly breathe in and out without assistance was also gone my ability to communicate anything beyond a Neanderthal level grunt. My head felt like someone had stuck it in a vat of honey, and words were too big and complex to form in my brain or mouth.

It had all come on so quickly. And it was all my own fault.

*   *   *

It was a chilly, dry autumn afternoon in early October 2013 when we managed to navigate the steep one-way streets of the Seattle inner suburb of North Queen Anne where Joe's friends lived.

Earlier that day, we arrived in Seattle after five straight days of driving across the country from Philly, with Joe's clothes and small possessions crammed into his car. I had flown in to help him pack the rest of his things into the U-Haul we sent ahead and to say goodbye to his family before we set out to start our new life on the West Coast. The plan was to park his car at his friend's place for a few weeks while he then joined me back in Melbourne. I still needed to finalize my visa, be a bridesmaid in Anna's wedding, and pack up my stuff before moving to Seattle permanently.

"So, who are we meeting tonight again?" I asked Joe as the outskirts of Seattle came into view.

Despite all of us being on the same site where Joe and I had met, I hadn't interacted with these people before.

"Mia and her boyfriend and our other friend, Dan," he

repeated. "It will be good to see them. I've been online with Mia and Dan for years, but we've never met in person."

I'd heard enough stories to know they were all around Joe's age or a little younger and just as quick-witted. I hoped I would hold my own in their company. We parked the car in Mia's driveway, and I bounded up the steps following Joe to the second-floor apartment.

Don't fuck this up, Shayla! I thought as I reached their landing. *These are the people you are going to be hanging out with once you move here. Thank God for internet friends!*

Mia met us at the door. She was about my five-foot five-inch height, with a huge warm smile that lit up her face. I was relieved. I instantly liked her and was grateful for the friendly reception.

"Welcome to Seattle!" she cried and immediately hugged us both. Then, before we even stepped foot inside the door, she handed me what looked like a thin translucent balloon filled with swirling Cannabis vapor instead of oxygen.

Joe and I had talked about his experience with weed (and psychedelics), but this was the first time we had come across it together. I knew weed was legal in Seattle, and not wanting to reveal myself as the drug novice I truly was, I didn't question anything before I took a drag and handed the bag to Joe.

I mean, I wasn't a *complete* stranger to the stuff—having lived a year in Amsterdam—but truth be told, I barely touched it after a nasty incident in San Diego back in '96, where I got completely wasted on homemade hash brownies. I'd also had my limited share of (weak-ass) joints in my travels and a couple of bong hits in my uni years.

This time was my first with a vaporizer, though, and I could barely taste the distinct flavor. *I've got this*, I thought, figuring it was highly diluted, but to be sure, I took a moderately small inhale.

We followed Mia inside to meet the others. The plan was to hang out at their apartment for a bit before we all headed to a local upscale Italian restaurant for dinner. When we walked in, Dan was standing by the window, looking out at the view over Elliot Bay and turned to greet us enthusiastically.

Hearing the voices, Mia's boyfriend joined us in the living room. We all sat down, and they started talking at lightning speed, trying to catch up quickly on each other's lives and news since they had last checked in. Somehow, in the middle of the conversation, the vaporizer bag was passed around again, and still without any thought of consequences, I took another hit and handed it on.

Suddenly I started to feel lightheaded, and the edges of my vision went fuzzy. I lost the thread of the conversation and felt myself sinking deeper and deeper into the couch. Concerned, I reached out and tugged gently on Joe's sleeve. "What is it, babe?" he asked distractedly, turning to look at me briefly.

But I couldn't say anything and just shook my head, so he turned back and continued the animated conversation.

"This stuff is medical grade. It's called AK47," I heard Mia say. "You need to have a medical marijuana license to purchase it, and it's only available to get from a dispensary." *Yeah, right. I'll bet it's called AK47 because it makes your head explode,* I thought to myself through my ever-increasing brain haze.

I have no idea how long we sat there before we made the move to go to the restaurant. It was all I could do to just smile and nod at everyone, hoping nobody would notice I wasn't saying anything.

When we all got up to go, I grabbed Joe's hand and hung on to it as we navigated down the stairs to the waiting car.

Thankfully, they all had so much to catch up on that the conversation on the short ride to the restaurant flowed around me.

By the time we pulled up and everyone got out, I felt like my limbs belonged to someone else and were no longer under my control. I attached myself like a limpet to Joe and hung on for dear life to his hand as we navigated across the busy street to the restaurant and started following the others in the door. Just as we got inside, I tugged harder on the back of Joe's shirt.

He turned to ask what it was, and this time caught the look of the rising desperation in my face. I stood there and slowly shook my head. Correctly assessing the situation, even though this was the first time he had ever seen me high, he promptly took me by the elbow and led me outside to a quiet stoop a couple of doors down the street.

Again, I had no concept of time and couldn't tell you how long we sat there, with me trying to breathe and Joe texting the others to let them know what had happened. They were waiting at the table with water and menus and were wondering where the hell we had gone.

"You were literally right behind us in the restaurant one minute, and then the next, you'd vanished!" Dan said when we were still laughing about it a year later. "We had no idea what was going on."

Eventually they found us. "Oh my god, Shayla! I'm so sorry!" Mia exclaimed when she saw me. "I feel so bad! I didn't mean to break you!" she continued, as if she was in any way to blame.

My eyes were glassy and my focus wandered, but I had by that time rallied enough to be able to stand up. "No. No… me," I managed to get out, trying unsuccessfully to shake my head. By now, my high-ness was coming in waves. I'd reach peak THC potency and be completely unable to function before momentarily dipping back down into a befuddled toddler-level mastery over my brain and body.

The consensus from the group had been to go back to Mia's place and not worry about dinner.

"No, don't. D—" I said haltingly, still struggling with the basic mechanics of speech. I was mortified. I didn't want to ruin everyone's night. We were looking forward to going to this restaurant, and reservations were hard to come by.

Somehow, I made it through the rest of the evening at the Thai restaurant we instead found close by. While everyone ate and talked around me, I sat propped up against the wall in the corner, unable to contribute to the conversation, with my fork stuck midway between my mouth and my plate.

I'd love to say that was the end of it and Joe and I went back to our hotel, slept, and woke up fresh the next day, but it didn't work out that way. At least, *I* didn't sleep. I was still so high that I was periodically forgetting how to breathe.

"Ha!" Joe snorted. "No, I'm not taking you to the hospital. I promise you it won't help. There is nothing they can do. You just have to wait it out," he replied to my naive request to seek medical attention. "You are fine. You are just really, *really* stoned," he said after a few hours, starting to get tired and frustrated. "It will wear off, I promise. Just go to sleep." But as much as I wanted to comply, I couldn't get my brain to switch off. I spent the night with my thoughts alternating between racing around my head in endless loops of half formed nonsense, to being stuck as if trapped in stodgy cold rice pudding. I didn't know what to do with my alien body, all tangled limbs and pounding chest. My tongue was a thick, dried out filet mignon in my parched mouth, and I constantly had to get up to drink more water and then pee.

The next morning, we checked out of the hotel at the

last possible moment. With hours to kill before our 5:00pm. flight back to Melbourne, we decided to have lunch at a burger joint before heading to the airport. By the time we got there it was about midday, and I still wasn't fully sober. My breathing had finally normalized, but my chest still ached and my head was a tug toy being randomly shaken by a puppy. I sat quietly, slumped in my chair, and half-heartedly picked at my fries.

Mia texted to check in and tell me again how bad she felt about what happened. *What did she have to be sorry for? It was all me.* Joe started to worry that we weren't going to make our flight. I didn't even know it was possible to still be high seventeen hours later and had no idea when it would be over.

Thankfully, our concerns were unfounded. By the time we got to the airport, I was able to think and move more normally. We got through airport security and made our way to our first flight to LA. I sat down, exhausted, and finally caught my breath.

Wow! Way to go, Shay! I told myself in disgust. *That's definitely one way to make a memorable first impression. Is this who I am now? Is this who I want to be? Someone who needs babysitting whenever she goes near weed? I'm sure that's the opposite of who Joe thought I'd be. Who am I kidding? I'm not in my twenties this time round. I have to go at my own pace and slow the fuck down. As lovely as they were about it all, I'm never getting high with them again. I'm going to need to find some other way to connect and make friends.*

By the time Joe and I returned a few weeks later to settle in properly to Seattle and we saw them all again, my self-recrimination had abated. I did do weed around them again, but I did it because I wanted to for other reasons, not because I was still trying to fit in. For at least a few years after that night, we all laughed about that incident but also found many more things to bond over, and I found I was more than capable of keeping up with the conversation when I was sober.

CHAPTER 9

Portion Control

———

Every self-help book I've ever read and every therapy I've ever done has taught me that I need to learn to listen to my own inner voice and trust that I want, and know how, to heal myself. I have the tools inside me to become whole again if I just let myself do it.

But for all my time as Mitch and almost a decade of being Shayla, despite all the Co-Co sessions and other forms of therapy I tried, I didn't let that voice be heard. I just ignored it, pushed it down, and smothered it with food, hoping it would shut up and go away. I knew letting that voice out of its box meant letting all the others out too, and I didn't want to listen to the voice of me from when I was six and in that closet.

I didn't want to listen to twelve-year-old me, terrified and shaking in the bedroom of our house in Ferntree Gully, where I heard Dad rage at Mum and Cherie and then punch a hole in the wall.

I ignored ten-year-old me who got hit with the broom handle by Dad when Maurice and I broke the antique etched-glass living room door after slamming into it when we were fighting over the TV remote.

I shut down the part of me who was six or seven and trembling with fear out the back of the house, while inside, and I still have no idea why, Dad exploded at Mum and smashed my Royal Doulton Baby Bunnykins plate set. He destroyed all but the one saucer I'd managed to grab before I ran out, clutching it tightly to my chest.

Those parts and more screamed inside my heart and head, including the ones that came later and especially after Dad's suicide. I shoved them back into their cold, dark cells, numbed them with an excess of food to keep them silent, and reinforced the containment defenses.

I wasn't capable of hearing them yet.

* * *

I learned early on in my life that barriers are good, so I tried my hardest to put one around my periphery. Any kind of food was socially acceptable heroin, and sugar was crack to me. Food was always there, dulling my senses and giving me protective fat to hide behind.

By the start of 2014, my weight started to climb again. I knew what that meant. I knew as much as I wanted to shut them out, I could no longer ignore all the silent screaming inside my head. My own inner voices competed with my dad's over what I should do next. Even if my conscious mind was turning a blind eye to what was going on inside my par-frozen heart, my subconscious still drove me toward opening each Pandora's box to peek inside.

By that stage, I'd learned so much about psychedelics' beneficial effects on helping heal trauma that I was determined to give it a go and see what they could do for me.

My problem was I was the poster child for the "Just Say No" campaign. My dad's, not Nancy Reagan's. Not unlike the official war on drugs, his was a deliberate smear campaign of misinformation and propaganda designed to confuse and control. My father wanted nothing to do with drugs of any description, and he made damn sure that I didn't either. Hell, he barely even drank. Growing up, beer went stale in our fridge, and he only occasionally had a glass of vodka or schnapps with Uncle Karl.

I don't know if it was because Dad was scared I'd become addicted or maybe because he knew how powerful and mind-expanding psychedelics could be. It was the last thing he wanted for me. You know, independent. Free-thinking. Open, connected to the universe and a master of my own destiny. He made sure I knew of all the possible unpleasant consequences getting caught high would mean. It was right up there on my Good Little Girl list of forbidden things.

It wasn't like I was offered cocaine as a kid, but I was around weed and probably all types of pills. In my head, however, having a few puffs of a joint as a teenager or a hit off a bong at university were just mild forays into the realm of rebellion and not meant to be major incursions into enemy territory.

Not surprisingly, it took some convincing for me to try anything more than weed. I'd had it a few more times since I'd been in Seattle and could take it or leave it. But as I was already aware of my food issues and my addiction to sugar, I was worried I might like psychedelics too much and not be able to stop.

I talked to friends about my concerns, and they set me straight. "Are you serious? No. Psychedelics are not addictive. You don't have to stress about that. That's just more bullshit from people who don't know anything trying to give them a bad rap." That was the consensus, which aligned with the results of my research. At that stage I hadn't yet read

Michael Pollan's book *How to Change Your Mind: What the New Science of Psychedelics Teaches Us About Consciousness, Dying, Addiction, Depression, and Transcendence*, but when I did, it completely aligned with my experience. I highly recommend anyone who is interested to learn more about this topic to read the book or watch the Netflix series.

It was late 2014 before I had a chance to put my desire into action. Joe and I lived downtown in our lovely two-bedroom apartment on the sixteenth floor. We had walls of windows, and to the south, we looked out at the gorgeous views of Mount Rainer; to the west, we could see through the buildings to snippets of the sun setting into the Puget Sound.

It was early afternoon when we got some mushrooms and made them into a tea, steeping the dried-up stems and caps until they became rehydrated, soft, and spongy. We used lemon juice to help convert the psilocybin to psilocin (the active psychedelic component), which made it react faster but for a shorter duration. Even though I was warned about what the effects could be, I still had no idea what I was really getting myself into. Given the way I reacted to weed previously, I should have been prepared for what happened that night, but I wasn't.

This adventure was totally different than anything I'd ever experienced before. Now, I know I should have had way less than I did, but I was unsure of the potency or the right portion. Joe gave me half of what he had, but in retrospect, I should have halved it again.

After forty minutes, my head started to feel fuzzy around the edges; not just my vision, but my whole brain and then my body. Suddenly I experienced the world through multiple Instagram filters. The shadows around me deepened almost to black, and the highlights burned bright white. I lost my peripheral vision and could only focus front and center. At first, I felt a bit tingly, which wasn't too unpleasant, but then I started getting a bunch of saliva in my mouth and my stomach went queasy.

Almost immediately I knew I had to vomit and made my way cautiously to the bathroom, arriving just in time.

Somehow, some time, I made my way back to the couch. I climbed on and burrowed my way in the back amongst the cushions. I sat there with my hands over my face, completely mute, with my virgin synapses totally overloaded.

I tried to look out at the city lights and the fading sunset, but all I got was a blur of yellows and bright blues, swirled with flashes of greens and reds. My brain was a canvas, and the psilocin was Photoshop. It was playing with the pixels, setting their intensity and saturation levels too high, and fiddling with the hue and contrast values.

After the session was done, I lay in bed, exhausted. I gave Joe a trip report the next morning.

"I just shut down. It was overwhelming, chaotic, and unpleasant. I felt sick and out of control."

"Yeah, it can be like that." He responded sagely. " But I'm not surprised. Everyone is different. Getting the portion right the first time can be tricky."

"I saw lots of pretty visuals, "I continued, " But nothing that made sense. Nothing in the way of healing insights. I'm kinda bummed, actually. I guess it isn't for me. If I want to continue with plant medicine, clearly I'm just going to have to learn how to handle my weed."

* * *

The weed culture is strong in Seattle. There are billboards beside the freeways advertising new dispensaries or pot shops, weed festivals, and 4/20 (Cannabis) day. People smoke or take an edible like they are drinking whiskey or smoking a cigarette. Bud-tending is a profession now, helping you choose among the multitude of products like you are ordering a custom car or your very own style of coffee at Starbucks.

"What kind of high do you want?" they ask when you go into the store.

"We have Sativa for helping you feel energized and creative or Indica for helping calm you down. Do you want a mix of THC to get you high and CBD to help you relax, or what about CBG, CBN, or any of the other active cannabinoids and terpenes to help with your pain or your mood?

"We have concentrates, resins, waxes, joints, edibles, or drinks; there are even weed-coated potato chips. You can take it topically in a cream or lingually under your tongue. Whatever you want in whatever dosage you need."

Back in 2013, I didn't even know what most of those terms meant. It was all so new and weird. I was naive about what weed was and what it could do. I thought if you had it more than once a week you were addicted. I also was so uptight about having it in the house. I still was under my Dad's influence and telling myself I would get in trouble.

Now I'm used to weed in all its forms being so prevalent and commonplace here it is almost as mundane as alcohol or caffeine. There is no thrill of illegality or worry of being caught. Now I know people take it responsibly and enjoy the ride.

After my epically disastrous attempt on my very first night in Seattle, even though I promised myself I wouldn't, I tried again. I persisted with trying to get a handle on weed over the next few years, mostly because I barely drink and (now I realize) it helped ease my social anxiety around new people and gave me a shared experience. Truth be told, when I got the dosage right I also found I liked how it felt.

It took me at least the next five years of experimenting with different ways of taking weed to find what worked for me. I've never been a smoker, so joints were out. I learned the hard way that even if it is secondhand smoke, it is just as potent.

I tried and failed pitifully at mastering the weed pen, which was just a scaled down version of Mia's volcano vaporizer that got me into so much trouble when we first met. I either took so little that it had no effect or I took so much that it almost knocked me out and my brain and speech was set at 0.25 speed. It was then a toss-up whether I would spend the night with a plastic bag beside me on the couch or sit cross-legged clutching the base of the toilet. That state was beyond high. When that happened, I leveled up and reached stoner status, and I can definitively say, I was not the least bit happy with the promotion.

What I did learn from those experiences, though, was if I was going to ingest, then I needed to be prepared. I needed to make sure I had taken care of the dog, cleared my schedule, and didn't have to drive for the rest of the day. Sometimes I even got the puke bowl at the ready, just in case.

Because of the unpredictability of my reaction and the time needed to recover, my weed usage has always been highly sporadic and restricted to holidays, weekends, and social events. Apart from how slow it made me, I was still worried that I might like it too much and lose control. I didn't want to use it as a crutch to numb out or, like I'd seen some people do, heavily self-medicate. I worried I was replacing my sugar with weed, but that concern was unfounded. For me, it never happened that way. For one thing, the more often I had it, the less effect it had. It self-regulated me to no more than one ten-milligram edible in a day. If I ever went beyond that amount, my reaction was never pretty. Being stoned was the opposite of where I wanted to be, as it shut down all my functions. Being high was where it was at. I eventually learned how to get my portion dialed in… and that's when the magic happened.

Unfortunately for me and those around me, at that stage, I wasn't yet able to appreciate or access that gift, as the part of myself capable of wielding it was still locked away; frozen in the dark, along with the rest of the things in my life I suppressed.

CHAPTER 10

Going into the Freeze

Just as I started writing this book, I did a short course on the biology of trauma held by health and trauma coach, Dr. Aimie Apigian. It opened my eyes, and I suddenly had the vocabulary to describe what had been happening to me all my life.

Dr. Aimie talks about how trauma affects the body and nervous system in her blog post, "The Shocking Impact of Chronic Stress and Trauma on Your Genetics."

She says, "When the body is exposed to high stress levels, the trauma gets stored in the nervous system. The effects of this stored trauma come out in your behavior patterns as an adult. Exposure to environmental stress has programmed your nervous system to stay in a state of survival mode. The nervous system goes into this survival state to protect the body. Being stuck in survival mode causes negative behavior patterns to develop, preventing you from living up to your full potential."

Thanks to her course, suddenly I had names for what I felt (or tried to). I always knew at a high level about the fight-or-flight response to danger and learned it was called the sympathetic state. I also knew from various therapies that emotion was stored in the body, but I didn't know on a biology level exactly what was happening to my nervous system, and how it was related.

She taught about the parasympathetic state, which is when you are calm, creative, relaxed, and feeling safe. It is supposed to be your default state when the danger has gone; however, the one she mentioned in her blog, the one where the body has been on high alert for way too long and can't sustain the fight-or-flight any longer, so it completely shuts down and is in survival mode? That was the freeze state, and I became its newest permanent resident.

*　*　*

In the earlier years of living in Seattle, there were many times I was frozen in place. I couldn't move. I felt so incapable of acting for myself that I could not have handled the logistics of transporting myself and my belongings back home or anywhere else. I was so emotionally overwhelmed by all the suppressed grief, re-stimulated emotional wounds, and stress that my nervous system shut down into a semi-permanent freeze.

"Joe, I owe you the hugest apology," I told him one morning when I started writing this chapter and thought about all that had transpired between us. "I'm sure I was a nightmare to live with when we first moved in together. I had no boundaries. I was not my best self. I hung on to you like you were the last tree standing in a hurricane."

His eyes narrowed when he looked at me, remembering those bad times. "No kidding! You resisted me *every* step of the way. Treated me like I was the enemy from day one. I couldn't do anything right. You *said* yes, but then your actions said *no*."

I drew a deep breath and blurted out, "You are right. I'm sorry! The truth is I was so scared you would leave me. So scared you would also die. I didn't want to get close and then lose you too. At the same time, I desperately needed you to love me, and even more, I needed to love you too."

Now I recognize I was doing to him what my father did to me: trying to hang on too tight, control every aspect of the situation, do everything I could to keep him and make him want to stay, while at the same time, not letting him get too close. It was such a push-me, pull-you dilemma. I was both attracted and repelled by the relationship and what real commitment meant.

Even though we really liked each other, and the relationship was still in its honeymoon phase, early on after moving in together, Joe and I found out the hard way that our living styles weren't exactly copasetic. I criticized him and nit-picked constantly, and defensive, he criticized back.

He loved being home, and I loved being out. He loved listening to podcasts or having the TV on loud, while I wanted music or quiet. He hated bright sunlight streaming into the apartment, and I craved the sun. He had his way of doing the dishes, and I had mine. You know, the usual little things that drive domestic partners insane.

Joe and I also didn't work well as a couple back then because we weren't ready. We didn't know each other. We didn't know how to communicate with, support, or read each other. We were so different. We didn't have any common background or culture or even enough real face-to-face time before I moved in with him.

Are you crazy, Shayla? I asked myself back then. And the answer was always *no*.

I'm not crazy that I did it. I trusted him. I knew that. But I *was* irresponsible. I should have said *not yet* when he asked me to move in with him. I should have stayed in Melbourne longer with my support network, grieved my mum, and got my head right first before jumping sight unseen into a new relationship, job, and country. But I didn't do that. I didn't give myself time. Mum's death threw me back into my default sympathetic mode of fight-or-flight, run and hide, and I took the first escape route I could find.

The longer we lived together, the longer the resentment on both sides built. It sparked a power struggle we couldn't seem to get out of. At times, it felt like the fights were never going to end.

Ordinarily, it would have been fine. If I was back in Melbourne and we were just dating, I would have retreated to my flat or gone to spend time at my girlfriends' places. But when I first arrived, I didn't have that outlet or escape. We lived in a 900-square-foot apartment, and there was nowhere private I could go to process or really be alone. I had no physical sanctuary anywhere else in Seattle. I didn't feel close enough to drop in on new friends unannounced. Even though now I'm sure it would have been fine, back then, I didn't feel like I could ask to spend the night on their couch.

* * *

One night in 2014, after a particularly awful fight, I raced outside just to get away. It was dark and pouring rain. It was almost midnight and I wanted to go somewhere, but I didn't know where to go or who to call. I ended up slumped against the window of the apartment building and started bawling. My fear, sadness, frustration, and grief came pouring out. Things had gotten so bad I'd finally tapped my well of repressed emotions. I created a temporary release for my trapped and locked up feelings, and they came gushing messily out. Once I'd released the pressure, my feelings were immediately submerged again. I'd taken the edge off, and those escaped emotions were once again corralled and put back into their cells.

Everyone knows suppressing emotions doesn't make them go away. It just triggered an inescapable downward spiral. By the time we moved to our own house in the middle of 2015 and lived there for a year or more, my state got progressively worse. The more Joe and I fought, and the more work was stressful and demanding, the more I retreated into the safe space in my mind. I was almost constantly dissociated, adding fuel to the fire.

I wasn't taking accountability for, or even remembering, the things I'd just said and done. Joe had a perfect memory, and it frustrated him no end, angering him even further.

"Are you trying to gaslight me?" he'd ask.

"But you literally just said that five minutes ago." "How can you not remember?"

"Are you kidding me right now?"

These were his all-too-common questions whenever I said "I don't know" or "I don't remember" to whatever it was he asked me at the time.

To make matters worse, I also spoke in draft, half-formed thoughts and ideas and often changed my mind. It drove Joe insane. To him, words mattered. Worst still, most of the time I was incapable of expressing what I really wanted, because I didn't even know what that was and had no idea how to ask for it, even if I did.

The constant fighting sent me further down the spiral and back to being little and powerless, and I'd disappear into my head even more. When I couldn't retreat and felt backed into a corner, I'd kick into fight mode and come out verbally swinging. I once threw a yellow pepper at Joe's head from across the room in my heightened frustration, and once I even smashed a plate onto the counter. Joe once slammed and broke the microwave door, but usually it would just devolve into screaming sessions on both sides, although never to name-calling.

One of those yelling matches escalated in early 2015 on a Saturday afternoon. We were in the car on our way back home from looking at yet another house that we couldn't afford or would get outbid on. We were exhausted and at a breaking point. We had been house-hunting for about ten months straight by that stage. I'd been to so many "Open for Inspections" that Jimi Lou, my real estate agent, became one of my close friends.

We reached downtown and were a few miles from our apartment when Joe and I got into an argument about something to do with the house. I don't even remember what it was about now, but I'm sure it stemmed from the fact that I wanted the house and Joe probably did not. My strong desire to nest was something I'd brought to Seattle with me and was still trying to achieve.

His voice got louder, and I raised mine to shout over his. My heart raced, pounding hard in my chest. Then something kicked me out of fight and into flight mode.

I couldn't meet his eyes, and my face was set in a mask of avoidance. I retreated as far away from him toward my door as possible. We pulled up to a stoplight, and without warning, I undid my seatbelt and bolted out of the car. Joe was initially too stunned to react and then yelled at me through the window, "Are you crazy? Get back in the car!" But I couldn't. Instead, I put my head down, turned away, and walked back to our apartment.

I couldn't fight in such close proximity. I needed space. I needed distance. I needed the safety of barriers and physical protection.

It wasn't even Joe I was fighting with or frightened of. It was the prime directive in my mind, running its usual route through my default neural pathways. My etched-in way of thinking.

Anger = trouble and *trouble = pain.*

Our arguments were a sign I made him unhappy, and to me, that equaled unsafe.

Anyone else could sit down and talk about the issues and hash it out, but I couldn't. My wiring was too strong. I was deep inside the closet in my mind, projecting all my terror and fear of reprisal onto Joe outside. To be clear, I was never under any kind of physical threat. Most of what was going on wasn't even in the present. I was just too triggered to know the difference.

Be the good little girl. Stay safe. Survive.

The technique which worked so well for me after my father died, *move, distract, do*, wasn't possible now. I couldn't run away, and there was nowhere to hide.

My response to the stress and fighting was what I did as a child. I tried to be what I thought Joe wanted me to be when I couldn't have been more wrong. I reverted to fawning to keep me safe and became the good little girl again.

I hid once more all the parts I had previously released as Mitch that I thought were now getting me in trouble. Any part that fought back, any part that was independent or rebellious, any part of me that made me stand out or otherwise might draw attention, I cut off at the pass. My creative, feminine, and adventurous side got caught in the crossfire. Eventually I put all of them, and even more for good measure, back into archival in ice and reverted to being Michelle.

*   *   *

The freeze process was gradual; so subtle at first, I didn't even notice. In truth, it probably started with Mum's cancer diagnosis, but it really hit the gas pedal around the end of 2017, with a progressive loss of self-esteem. I stopped wanting to exercise, and my weight continued to steadily climb. I stopped going for walks and exploring my surroundings or doing things for myself. Over the years, I'd deferred more and more decisions to Joe and given away more and more of my power. My work was getting harder. I was on a new team and felt like a fraud when I didn't deliver what they asked for. By then Joe had been studying for a few years and was home literally *all* the time. I needed space to think. As much as I had been avoiding it, I needed to grieve. I needed to process my loss and what my life looked like now that I didn't have any parents, or for that matter, any children either.

I wasn't coping. I had friends, and they were helping, but the downward trajectory was too compelling. By this point, the freeze was out of my control. I was fighting my biology, not my will.

My brain and body gradually powered down. I was the Energizer Bunny running out of battery. One thing about being in the freeze response is it turns off all your motivation. I had no curiosity or drive for anything other than eating and watching TV.

Joe would say to me, "Shay, why don't you have a hobby? You don't seem to be interested in anything."

It was true. I'd get excited about the start of something and enthusiastic about the big picture, but as soon as it got into the nitty gritty and took more effort to dive deeper, I'd get overwhelmed and power down again.

Any joy was fleeting. Any pleasure, temporary.

What I hadn't realized up until I started doing plant medicine was that most of my life I'd been wandering around the world with my nervous system permanently set somewhere around the sympathetic state of DEFCON level two or three. It would very rarely go back down and stay at level five (my parasympathetic state), no matter how hard I tried.

Since 2013, however, circumstances slowly built to the perfect storm, until my nervous system snap froze at the nuclear DEFCON level one. As I moved into 2018, my freeze went from a few flurries to a full-blown blizzard. My body was in Seattle, but my heart may as well have been in the Arctic—no, more like Siberia, where they sent you to live out your days trapped in the ice and snow instead of sending you to an actual prison.

I'd reached the tipping point where every day more and more of my heart and soul became trapped in carbonite and more parts of me were frozen away than were accessible. I was left working off a limited range of emotions.

Depression, anxiety, and fear.

I wanted to quit my job and try something different, but my visa process meant I couldn't leave, and because of it, I became beholden to my employer. We'd also bought a new house and then a dog, so instead of making my life easier to uproot, I had dug myself in deeper.

Suddenly there was no escape from everything that scared me. I was tethered to the spot and felt like the only way out was down.

Without even thinking about where I'd seen this dark path lead my father, I slipped into excavation mode. I gathered up all the grief, shame, panic, and despair and honed it until it became the sharp edge of my spade. I began digging my misery pit, right through my frozen core.

CHAPTER 11

The Misery Pit

I never really thought before about what it feels like to have an emotional breakdown; a literal, public, at the office, snot-nosed, tears streaming and blood pumping in your ears type of breakdown of control over your emotions.

I had never *really* cried at work before. I had never been ready to storm out of an office and quit on the spot. I had been stressed and under pressure and on tight deadlines before, but I had never reached this breaking point. I had never been rock bottom in my pit before. Something had to give, and at that point, it was my work.

"I don't know what you want from me!" I erupted at my manager one morning when he critiqued my work.

I was a child again and being yelled at by Dad for being lazy and not doing my chores.

Work = safe. An echo of Dad's voice repeatedly whispered in my ear.

I was doing everything I could, and it still wasn't enough.

Klaxons started going off inside my head. This was the epitome of getting in trouble.

* * *

While the lead up to digging my misery pit was gradual, I can tell you the precise moment I reached its bedrock. It was November 2018, right after Thanksgiving.

As I progressed further down my pit, my high-stress job, normally well within my capacity, was now too much to bear. It consumed all and more of the resources I could give it. Outside the pit, the winter rain, cold and endless dark were relentless. I was failing, and I was falling apart. I felt like I had no options, no escape, and no safety net to catch me and stop my free fall.

Reaching out to anyone took effort and was too hard. Getting out of bed and going to work, or looking after myself, the dog, or the house, took effort and was too hard. I lost the desire to do anything and stopped any forward momentum in my life. I was frozen in place.

My thoughts turned darker and darker until the darkness got so dense and suffocating I was willing to do almost anything to be free of it. I was sinking fast, and if I didn't do something different very soon, I would drown. I didn't want to see only one way out of the pit; one way to feel like I had any control over my life.

To do what my father had done.

* * *

Being born my father's daughter, I already had the tools and resources I needed for creating my own pit of misery. I'd spent all my childhood watching Dad digging ever deeper into his depression and trying to drag me down into it with him. "The pit," as I liked to call it, was different than the ice prison of cells in my heart; each cell a Pandora's box holding my suppressed emotions and my "dangerous" parts of self, frozen and locked away.

The pit was new. It was the part of my soul that should have been the light behind my eyes. It was the core of who I was and what I believed about myself. It was the corroded hole through the center of my self-worth, self-respect, and self-love, excavated by all my dark thoughts and feelings.

Previously in my life there hadn't really been a pit—more like pock marks and puddles on the surface of my heart. Localized points of suffering that eroded away my self-esteem, but now, all those previously isolated incidents of hurt and injury to my sense of self had pooled together in a swirling dark morass of grief, fear, and heartbreak and became more toxic and hollowed out more of my heart every day.

When it came to digging my pit, I found out the conveyancing had already been done and the paperwork signed. After Dad died, I cleared the surface and marked out the borders. All it needed was the right push to set me in motion. Then, after Mum died, I started digging its foundations, and by early 2018 my excavation got going in earnest.

Even during those hardest times as Michelle and early on as Mitch, when I had the most parts of myself locked away, I somehow managed to keep smiling and finding some joy and zest for life—at least on the surface. Back then, if I was sad, scared, or lonely, I usually didn't think about it too long or hang out there. I managed to distract myself with school or work, parties, bike rides or travel, and (mostly) unrequited romantic love.

This time, however, after each negative interaction with Joe or at work, I couldn't help but dwell on it. By mid-2018, I'd rented excavation equipment and given up on the spade. Every time Joe was unhappy or we got into a fight, I dug deeper and harder, through the permafrost, and into the pit, faster than ever before.

It kept me so preoccupied that I didn't have time to miss anyone. I didn't have time to actually *feel* sad. I didn't have time to feel the overwhelming loss of my mother, my home, my community, and my youth all at the same time. All those things I ignored were desperately clanging their cups silently against their cell doors begging for my attention. All I heard as I dug were those scared, angry, and anxious voices from parts of me left free to roam, while all the other parts were trapped and frozen. *Don't get too comfortable,* they warned me from the shadows. *Don't let your guard down. You know something bad is going to happen. It always does.*

I heard them subliminally with the volume up loud. *You don't deserve love. You are unlovable. Useless, fat, lazy. No good at anything. No wonder Dad checked out. And now you don't even have Mum. You are not worth sticking around for. You know you deserve to be alone.*

I needed to turn them down, but I couldn't. I was so distressed by everything going on that I became completely subsumed by the pain. My energy was so drained by suppressing those voices and being in survival mode that I couldn't function with anything else.

I didn't need digging equipment anymore. The floor of the pit was quicksand, and I was sinking fast.

Every negative thought I ever had about myself became amplified in the dark. I rehashed how bad a person I was. I relived all my worst deeds: shame at leaving my dad, along with all my guilt at not reading his book while he was alive and failing as his daughter when he needed me the most. They were ankle bracelets weighing me down, making it even harder to pull myself up and out of the pit.

Joe kept telling me, "Just do *it.*" "Get over *it.*"

"Move on or change *it*."

Whatever *it* was that I didn't like about myself or he didn't like about me.

But I couldn't. I didn't know how. I couldn't access the thought patterns, beliefs, energy, or capacity to make the change, because the parts of me which had all those resources to do so were frozen, incapacitated, drowned out, and locked away. I had to find a way to unfreeze and hear them first before I could access their gifts of action.

I thought I would be trapped in that misery pit forever. Its walls were too steep and slippery. I had no foot or hand-hold, ladder to climb, or rope of faith or hope with which I could haul myself up and out; just more sadness, darkness, fear, grief, and self-hatred.

I tried to get a therapist, but I struggled to find one who took my insurance and accepted new patients. I wanted to do Co-counseling, but that was the rub. It required a "co." I didn't have my community here. I tried to find someone in Seattle, but it didn't work out.

Thankfully Jlynn, one of the co-counselors in Hartford I'd adopted as a mother of choice, was there for me. We did video sessions every fortnight, and it was my lifeline. Between work pressure and lack of energy, it was all I could manage. Forget trying to call home. The time difference, added with busy schedules, was a logistics nightmare. It was a rare occasion when the stars aligned and I managed to chat to close friends or Cherie. I'd text more regularly with people than I would talk, but that didn't satisfy my craving for face-to-face connection.

Joe and I became closer with a small gang of friends who lived, or used to, in our old apartment building. We did Friendsgiving and rooftop BBQs and Halloween parties. We started going camping together more regularly. I became especially close with my friend, Britt. When we could, we walked and talked. I met up with other girlfriends and had birthday dinners or went to the movies. When Joe and I weren't fighting, we met up with friends and had good times.

And all of it helped–just not enough.

Happy wasn't allowed to last.

By this time, I was so far down the misery pit that I needed a longer rope. There were too many barriers the outside love and support had to get past to reach me and haul me out. I was dug in too deep. I was constantly buried by my crap. As soon as I came up out of the pit for a breath of fresh air, something at work or home, or especially on the news, would send me right back down again.

It was the first time in my life I have ever been that depressed, and it scared me. Like, for real, *scared* me. I was having thoughts I didn't want to have.

I just want this to be over. I need a way out!

I don't know if Joe realized how dark my thoughts got during those days. How often I stood on the precipice of checking out; not necessarily out of life *just* yet, but definitely out of Seattle and our relationship.

Part of the problem was no one here really knew me at all, including Joe. They had no baseline. They didn't know how far off course I had gone. They didn't see my emotional decline, and I couldn't reach out to those who did. I was so ashamed of how I had become that I didn't want to admit to it or see it. I just retreated behind my fat and hid in the deepest, darkest hole in my mind I could find.

To make matters worse, during all this was when my body started really failing me. I don't know whether its decline was the cause or result of being in the pit or just another iron in the fire. I wanted to break the taboo and scream from the rooftops to anyone who would listen.

"Ladies, and those who love their ladies, *do not underestimate how much menopause can disrupt your life!*"

If you are one of the lucky ones who just skated through unscathed by hot flashes or night sweats or increased anxiety, I applaud you. But I wasn't. It destroyed me. I could no longer sleep. My hormones were *all* over the place. I was dizzy and had phantom period pain, sore boobs, and headaches. The worst was I didn't know if the mood swings, depression, and anxiety were from the stress or the hormones.

Of course, for me it all came at the worst possible time in my life. It was just another thing to deal with when I was already vulnerable and down. It was a double whammy to my self-confidence. I'd look in the mirror and not recognize who I saw.

Who is this old ass woman? I'd think when I'd catch an unexpected glimpse of my reflection.

Deep lines on my forehead wouldn't go away no matter how much cream I rubbed into my face. Annoying, stubborn white hairs wouldn't take hair dye no matter how many times I reapplied. Every joint and muscle ached. Persistent low-grade injuries I'd ignored for years were now hampering my quality of life. I'd limp getting out of bed first thing in the morning, and I dreaded walking the dog or doing any other kind of exercise.

I suddenly had a belly I could grab and lift with my hands.

Holy crap, where did that come from? The muffin top from hell!

Since I'd put on so much weight, I already hated my body, and then *wham!* I'd be sitting on the couch, or in the store, or even at work, and with absolutely no provocation, I'd spontaneously combust. I felt disgusting and embarrassed and the complete opposite of sexy and attractive. I couldn't stand being touched by either Joe or the dog, which meant the only source of comfort I got was from eating.

And then the inevitable happened, as it was bound to do. I reached a point where I was so deep in the pit I couldn't sustain my façade. Outside of the pit, my life crumbled. At work, usually my safe haven of doing and distracting, I was going downhill faster than I could pull myself back up again.

As the team's user experience designer, figuring out how the application would work to best meet the needs of the users was my role. What they wanted from me was curiosity, creativity, and imagination; to think big and dive deep. To be fair, the job didn't change. I knew that's what they wanted from the outset and was what I signed on for, but my heart wasn't in it. I had nothing left in the tank to dedicate to the effort required to keep up with the workload. Those parts of me were now frozen solid.

* * *

"I'm done. I don't need this," I said, failing to fight back the tears. I stood up abruptly, ready to leave. "I quit."

I'd kicked straight into flight mode and I had to escape. My manager stopped me. "Wait, Shayla. Just take a breath. Let's go to lunch and talk about it first."

We were silent on the walk to the nearby restaurant and the time it took to wait for a table. I couldn't meet his eyes. We sat at the table, and he asked me what I wanted to do moving forward.

I inhaled and tried to think. My mind was blank. All I wanted was to be anywhere but there and feeling how I was feeling.

"I need a break. I need to get away. Reassess what I'm doing and where I'm going," I eventually told him.

Then something pinged deep down inside.

"I want to take a three-month sabbatical," I said, meeting his gaze.

"If you're sure that's what you want, we can arrange that," he replied.

Finally, from all the way down the very bottom of my pit, that self-healing inner voice inside me made herself heard. I had reached bottom, and there was no other avenue of escape I wanted to take. Now the only way to go was up. I knew I needed to do something drastic to change.

Finally, I was ready to listen to what all my locked-away parts had to say. I also knew I was going to need help unlocking the cell doors and defrosting the parts so I could revive them enough to talk. I needed to turn on the light in my heart.

For that, I knew I needed plant medicine. I needed ayahuasca.

CHAPTER 12

Aya-what-a?

The first time I heard of ayahuasca was at a party in Melbourne during the Mitch era, so around 2008 or '09. I was chatting to this girl who had just gotten back from Peru, and she told me about her experience. It sounded awful. Projectile vomiting and diarrhea... in the jungle, with limited plumbing. But the part that stuck with me, and a decade later made me decide to want to try it, was the spiritual awakening and healing she professed to have gained from her brave, and brief, sojourn into the shamanic world. Always with an ear out for any possible avenue of a healing opportunity, I was intrigued; grossed out and apprehensive, but intrigued.

It was that initial ear worm of an idea that had my ears prick up when I heard more about ayahuasca as a highly effective, healing, native plant medicine for PTSD, addiction, anxiety, and depression. I believe the podcast Joe and I were listening to which gave me this information was an episode of *The Joe Rogan Experience*; possibly the one where he interviewed Rick Doblin, the founder and executive director of the Multidisciplinary Association for Psychedelic Studies

(MAPS), but I can't say for sure. We listen to a lot of podcasts on road trips. It's kinda our thing.

Knowing Joe Rogan, though, it's a pretty good bet it was him, because back when we used to listen to his show, he had to mention on every episode 1) that you should give up gluten; and 2) how beneficial psychedelics and plant medicine are for curing every type of emotional malaise. Okay, to be fair, it wasn't *every* type of emotional issue, but it was definitely the ones resonating with me.

After my emotional breakdown at work, I knew I needed an intense intervention. If that intervention meant throwing up into a bucket in the jungle, I was desperate enough to try it. Therapy alone clearly wasn't cutting it, and I know there were probably medical approaches I could have taken, but the idea of being on pills did not appeal to me.

I started listening to more podcasts about ayahuasca and researching it on the internet. I found out from Ayahuasca. com that "ayahuasca is a hallucinogenic drink made from the stem of the ayahuasca vine (*Banisteriopsis caapi*). The ayahuasca drink is sometimes, but rarely, made from the ayahuasca vine alone; almost invariably other plants are added. These additional ingredients are most often the leaves of any of three *compañeros*, companion plants—the shrub *chacruna,* the closely related shrub *sameruca,* or a vine variously called *ocoyagé, chalipanga, chagraponga,* and *huambisa.*"

The more I read, the more I wanted to do it. I found out that just like Co-counseling and even weed, it wasn't for everybody, but it was suitable for me. It was non-addictive, spiritually awakening, and should be administered by a genuine shaman in an authentic ceremony where you feel safe. I didn't want a commercialized, culturally appropriated, new-age version people did just to get high. I was going to try my hardest to find a real shaman and do a real ceremony, in the most respectful way I could, no matter where it was and how much of an inconvenience it would be to get there.

I researched multiple places offering ceremonies, all of which were outside of the US, and settled on one in Mexico. It is not lost on me that as much as I didn't want to be a spiritual tourist, the place I ended up was at a resort and not in the wilds of Peru. However, I did find an experienced shaman who lived and studied with other shamans for many years in Peru and Mexico and was a healer, not just a western psychedelic sherpa. I have traveled to many places, and most of them on my own, but I don't speak Spanish and had never been to Mexico before. "It's too much. I don't know if I can do this," I told Joe after reading out the details of the trip. Even though I was on an upward trajectory, I was still submerged in the pit and struggling with action and confidence. "I'm already stressed out enough about doing ayahuasca without grappling with the logistics."

"I'll come. I'll do it with you," Joe said, clearly seeing my hesitation and not wanting me to back out.

I'm not sure if it was more for his level of comfort or mine, or if he was just curious about trying ayahuasca, but either way, I gratefully accepted his offer of travel companionship and let go of at least that anxiety.

We contacted the shaman, and his wife who assisted with the ceremony. They gave us a very detailed health and background questionnaire to fill out and carefully explained what to expect from the experience and the preparation diet required. I breathed a sigh of relief, knowing we were in professional hands.

* * *

As it turned out, circumstances conspired to make it a major inconvenience to get there. Three years after listening to that first podcast, Joe and I made it through a rare Seattle snow-storm, grounded planes, missed connections, and then more re-routed and majorly delayed planes to at last arrive in Mexico. The day after that, we navigated the last leg of our journey to finally arrive at our destination two days late.

The resort was a purpose-built, eco-friendly, spiritual yoga and health retreat center and was carved out of the jungle by hand. Cream-colored rooms were cradled in terraces with irregular stone and cement steps leading up the side of a steep hill. Every level had basic guest rooms with adjoining bathrooms, and the large communal kitchen and dining space were at the very top. Lush plants and numerous brightly colored flowers crowded the spaces between the buildings and wherever the diligence of the gardeners couldn't reach. "Here you go. This is you," a friendly resort worker said, dropping our bags at the door and handing us a key.

He'd led us about halfway up the hill to a simply appointed room with a queen-size bed under mosquito netting and a plain wooden dresser pushed against the inside wall. Opposite was a low outside wall completely open to the elements up to the thatched rooftop. It made the room feel spacious and airy like a giant partially covered balcony. A large hammock hung from the ceiling by the open wall, perfectly positioned to take advantage of the stunning panorama laid out below. It had uninterrupted views of the canopy of palms and other tropical trees interspersed amongst the rooms on the lower terraces and the glittering blue water of the bay in the distance.

After we got ourselves settled into our room, we went up to the communal area to meet the others. The rest of the participants were mostly American, a mix of men and women, aged between mid-twenties to late fifties, some couples and some alone. A few had done the ceremony before and came back after positive experiences, but out of the ten of us, most were doing this for the first time. We quickly bonded over our nervous anticipation of what the experience would hold.

Even as I stood in the dining room chatting to the other participants, I felt the anxiety of our travel delays melting away. I became more present to my surroundings and my heart opened to what was about to come. The group and the shaman had all graciously agreed to rearrange the schedule so we wouldn't miss out on the orientation session or the first ceremony due to our travel nightmare, so after a brief but warm welcome and introduction, we found our way to the room where the ceremony would be held.

*   *   *

By the time dusk fell, I found myself sitting in a room similar to our own but much larger at about fifteen feet wide, with curved adobe walls, a thatched roof also open to the sky at one end, and a faded, rose-colored painted concrete floor with a huge crack down the center.

Large and intricately sewn Shipibo tapestries hung on the walls, their ancient Peruvian style depicting ayahuasca interpretive designs. I think the pattern looked like a 2D version of our gray matter, with its squiggly pathways and juncture points echoing the fissures and grooves of the brain. *I'm really going to do this*, I thought, looking around the room and giving myself a quick pep talk. *Shayla, there is no backing out now!*

Arranged around the edges of the room were fourteen

people, myself and Joe included, sitting at little comfort stations set up with green vinyl backjacks against the walls. Each had a couple of folded multicolored striped sarape blankets and yoga cushions, and, with disquieting hints of what was to come, two-liter orange or purple plastic buckets. Toilet paper rolls were scattered strategically within arm's reach around the room.

Four of those setups were clustered close together at one side of the room, where the shaman, his wife, and two apprentices sat with the others spaced out evenly around the walls. Situated in front of the shaman was a little ceremony altar. Set upon a thick blanket was an assortment of items, laid out with deliberate and practiced care.

The altar consisted of sacred objects, including wooden prayer beads, a much-creased and evidently loved black-and-white photo of the Dalai Lama, feathers, and various crystals and little buddha statues. Beside them were candles and lighters and a variety of plastic vials, droppers, and jars containing other integrative medicines including rapé, sananga, and mambe. The ayahuasca brew was in a 1.5-liter water bottle on the right-hand side of the altar. The mixture was a deep crimson brown and left an oily residue on the inside of the clear plastic container.

I couldn't draw my eyes away from the assortment of objects. I had an intense fascination and curiosity about what each of those items would be used for and, on a scale of one to ten, just how unpleasant they would be and how many expelled bodily fluids would be involved.

Please, please, just let me get to the toilet without soiling myself first! I silently prayed.

There is not a lot I am grateful for about those times when I got way too stoned and either threw up or felt my cognitive abilities completely dissolve, but they did at least give me a quiet comfort in that moment, when I sat waiting for the ceremony to start, that I had been in a dissociative state before, and as unpleasant as it was, I survived.

*   *   *

People say Mother Ayahuasca calls to you, and I felt her call before I even took a sip. I felt it weeks before I arrived in Mexico, the minute I resolved to do the ceremony and started my cleansing preparatory diet. I felt her magic working backward from the future moment of ingestion, preparing me for healing and releasing my victim mentality's hold onto traumatic hot spots along my timeline, like a chiropractor removing tension by realigning a spine.

Sitting there, I knew I didn't have a choice. I knew I had to ensure continuity in my version of the space time continuum by taking the brew in this present, so my past and my future could be as Mother Aya ordained.

Despite all that, and even though I trusted this was exactly where I was supposed to be, I was still incredibly apprehensive. I knew I had to listen to my inner voices, but that didn't mean I was going to like what they had to say.

I took a deep breath, and as I let it slowly out, I forced that scared part of me to stand down.

From my vantage point of facing the open side of the room, I watched darkness push out the last vestiges of violet from the sunset sky. Candles were lit, eliciting a nervous and reverent hush to fall and elongated shadows to flicker around the pale curved walls. It was a balmy tropical night, but I shivered. Joe was sitting on his mat to my left, and our eyes met. He gave me a quick reassuring smile.

The shaman spoke up in his beautiful lilting accent. "We are about to start the ceremony. As a reminder, we ask you to adhere to the following rules for the duration. Number one: Once you have taken the brew, you cannot leave this room. If you need to go to the bathroom, raise your hand and one of the assistants will help you. But you cannot leave and go outside until we have all finished our session. We start together, and we end together.

"Number two: I understand you might experience some startling visions or bodily sensations during your journey, but please do everything you can to ensure you are as quiet as possible. Please respect other people's journey, and do not distract them with your own."

He continued, "I shall come around the circle, starting on my right, and will start by cleansing. I will ask you to think of your intention of what you want to ask Mother Aya, and then you will drink."

The shaman started quietly whispering a prayer I couldn't clearly hear and wouldn't understand even if I could. He lit a smudge stick and turned to the man sitting to his right in the circle and started waving the smoke over him with a feather. He lent in closely and said a prayer, asked him if he had his intention, and then offered him a drink of ayahuasca.

With every fiber of my being, I knew my intention: *I want to heal.*

That was it. Simple. You know, no small feat. Just complete emotional health and freedom from all types of pain. I wanted so desperately to be whole and complete again; in my body, in touch with and open to my feelings and emotions. I wanted to escape my misery pit and fill it with so much happiness and joy I could never fall down it again.

I was sixth in line. I watched Joe get his dose just before me and his face screw up at the taste. I knew it wasn't going to be pleasant, but I had done enough Chinese herbal medicine treatments in the past to know they all tasted like some variation of lawn clippings and garden mulch. When I got my taste, it was as I expected, but more bitter and oily.

Once we were all given a dose, the shaman returned to his seat and started chanting and singing some traditional Peruvian *Icaros*, the ancient healing songs to guide the medicinal journey.

Unfortunately, the scared, protective, and hesitant parts of myself were still in charge, and I didn't take a big enough dose of the ayahuasca the first night to fully go into an altered state. All I got for my trouble was purging, through voluminous amounts of vomiting, and a long and uncomfortable night sitting on the floor in the dark, watching and listening to others having awakening experiences.

What the fuck have I done? I thought as another wave of cramping and nausea twisted my guts.

I was conscious of being quiet, so I kept my groaning volume as low as I could. Thankfully the feeling didn't persist, and as soon as the waterfall of mostly fluid left my mouth and filled my bucket, the pain eased.

I was aware of someone to the right of me crying softly. Muffled sobs and gasps of air. Elsewhere in the room was indistinct breathing and sounds of purging and nose-blowing. I lay there, my body spent, listening to the shaman and his wife and son singing their medicine songs in Spanish and English, and then they moved into Hindu and Buddhist mantras and played the guitar. They took turns checking on the participants and making sure we had tissues, clean buckets, and anything we needed to be comfortable and safe.

Eventually, after what felt like an eternity but was about five hours, the shaman stopped playing and started to light candles. Everyone quieted down, and he invited us to sit up on our mats. After a while, we got up as a group and went outside to the large open deck used for yoga and stood in a huddle, looking at the stars. People talked excitedly about their experiences and shared what they saw. I disappointedly reported I had had no visuals or otherwise altered experience. After a while, we departed for our rooms and bed.

* * *

The next day was a rest day. We gathered at breakfast and excitedly dissected the events of the night before like relieved school children after an exam. It turned out I was not the only person without an intense reaction. This made me feel a little better, but I was still disappointed; mostly with myself. "Don't be disheartened," the shaman told me when I mentioned I didn't think it was working and how I felt like I was missing out. "It's not uncommon to only purge the first time, and even that is beneficial as the aya is still helping to heal you," he said reassuringly. "Next time, try taking a bigger dose."

I walked away from the conversation determined to do just that.

CHAPTER 13

My Rebirth Day

The third day of the retreat, after a short hike to the local waterfalls and a very limited, simple lunch, we assembled again in the ceremony room at dusk. As before, the shaman lit the candles and started his prayers. He again came around the circle asking for our intention, cleansed us with the smudge stick and puffs of tobacco, and offered us the sacred brew.

Tonight is the night when shit is going to get real, I promised myself.

I was determined this time. I thought again of my intention, which sounded more like a prayer. *I want to heal! I want to find peace and happiness. I want to listen to and know myself. I want to let go of my tether to Dad. I want to live for myself. Please, please, please, Mother Ayahuasca, help me. I can't do it on my own anymore.*

I let go of trying to control anything, conceded to the will of Mother Aya, then took a huge gulp of the bitter, herbaceous drink and gave myself up to the experience.

About thirty minutes or so later, I started to feel the nausea and familiar waves of abdominal cramping. After a few moments, I purged into my bucket and sat cross-legged on the floor, bent over on my mat with my head resting on my folded forearms.

My perception of my body gradually dissolved. I closed my eyes and saw light as bright as if I was standing in daylight outside. It was like a CGI movie was being projected onto the back of my eyeballs, and it was the most vivid, vibrant, immersive 3D movie I could ever imagine.

Suddenly I was floating in that space. I was flying. I was dreaming but was awake. I was infinite and paradoxically infinitely small. I was at one with the universe. I was part of the universe, and at the same time the universe was a part of me. It was all intertwined and seamless. It was like all my life I had been adrift in space, cut off from the source, and now I had just docked back into the mothership. I was home.

Here there was no fear, no angst, or anger or frustration, no concerns or desires, and no critical voices in my head. It was just peace and calm, and it was amazing.

That night, Mother Aya finally pulled back the curtain of obfuscation and inattention and showed me the true inner workings of my subconscious. She showed me my thoughts as benevolent snakes, of which I felt no fear. Their skins were alive and patterned, vivid with luminescent spectrums of black-lit fluorescent paint. They chased their tails, swallowing themselves and each other, in endless loops of writhing, prismed light and movement.

I dove into disappearing iterations of radiant fractal images that repeated and repeated on themselves, starting huge and becoming infinitesimally small. I became those images. I saw and became the snakes and then specks of cosmic dust in the form of DNA. They were the fabric of the universe. They were the fabric of me. They were woven into this incredible kaleidoscope of optical stimulus twanging my visual cortex and playing it like a harpsichord.

My conscious self was swept, spinning and gliding, down the chemically induced portal, until it was unceremoniously dumped out into a foam pit of visual imagery and symbolism. My attention was trapped and tethered to the wave of fading lucidity rippling along the side of the snake's body, inviting me to follow.

So I went where it led me. I was a guest in this world, and I let my subconscious thoughts be my guide. They carried me as if on a magic carpet, along the path to meet my own mind.

I went to where my curious self, and my proud self, and all the other exiled parts of myself were inexorably pulled back together by strong cohesive bonds; drawn together like stray droplets of glossy mercury, reforming back into the shimmery, technicolored brilliance from which they had once come.

For the first time, I saw my true, whole and complete, untarnished, original self; the self not inhibited or splintered by thoughts of pleasing anyone else or being anything else, just to survive; the self free to play and giggle and be silly, or sexy, or even angry, if I so desired. I saw what it was to be safe to just be me. *All* of me.

Inside of that experience, I completely lost all connection with my body. I lost all sense of space, time, and reality, the floor, and who or where I was. My identity and my ego dissolved, and it was just my consciousness finally aware of my subconscious.

With the cone of silence around my subconscious removed, I finally accessed it in all its multidimensional, surround-sound clarity. I could finally listen to what it was trying to tell me, and it had a lot to say. It spoke in all the voices of my jettisoned selves and my past lives. All the collective wisdom, all the collective love, flooded my body, my cells, and the receptors in my brain.

When I came back into my body hours later, I tried to remember and describe the experience to the other ceremony participants and to myself.

I remember saying something to the effect of, "Today is my rebirth day."

I was reborn that night. I know that might sound religious, but this wasn't anything to do with any organized religion's traditional concept of the divine. This was an awakening of my spirituality. And by spirituality, I mean getting in touch with my own spirit. I reconnected with my sense of self and my own innate ability to heal.

I was finally tuned in loud and clear to that part of me that wanted me back in one piece. It knew my self was meant to be once again perfect, whole, and complete. I just had to listen again to that inner voice; that gut intuition that all my life guided me and helped me to survive. That part of me had been trying everything it could to get me in the right places for the right reasons at the right times.

It helped Michelle hide when she couldn't run or fight back. It helped her adapt and change and abandoned parts of her where it needed to. It made her the good little girl and kept her safe.

It kept Mitch safe when she was traveling the world and testing the waters of her newfound freedom. It took her to therapists, body workers, and into sweat lodges.

And not least of all, it gave me, as Shayla, the courage to try plant medicine and persist in a relationship.

During the ceremony, that part of me opened like a parched cactus flower to a desert rainstorm and drank in the healing energy of the ayahuasca in huge thirsty gulps and started working in overdrive.

It had a lot of work to do. I had been shut down for so long, and that part had been so drowned out by the buzz of anxiety and critical directives in my head that its voice was reduced to a dry, raspy whisper—now it was turned back up to a roar.

*　*　*

As with the first night, after everyone completed their sessions, we grabbed our blankets and mats and headed outside to lay on the resort's yoga deck. We gathered and watched the multitude of stars jostling for room in the perfectly dark, cloudless jungle sky. Joe lay beside me, sharing a blanket, and we both silently processed our experiences from earlier that night.

"The real healing happens after the ceremony, when you integrate the learnings and gifts from your journey into your everyday life," the shaman told us in our original orientation session. "What you do here has the power to change your thought patterns, behavior, and beliefs and how you live your lives."

I completely believed him. Already I felt different. I had experienced profound shifts in my view of self and what I wanted for my life moving forward. Doing the ayahuasca gave me back my hope I would be okay. I would one day be able to heal and no longer have to hide.

The next day, we once again sat around a circle with the rest of the group, analyzing our journeys and sharing our learnings. I wasn't the only one who had had an incredible experience this time round. I'm happy to report that Joe had a positive experience and learned a lot about himself too. We talked about how deeply touched we were by our interaction with Mother Aya and what we learned about ourselves and our future paths.

I tried to describe to them how, in my journey, along

with parts of me I had long lost touch with, I had met my own version of Mother Ayahuasca.

To me, she was this constantly morphing creature, like an ever-changing chimera, surrounded by a rainbow-hued background of fractalizing thought snakes. She was both mythic and epic, but I had felt no fear or intimidation when I saw her. She had calmly and matter-of-factly answered my prayer from the intention and focus I had set for the session. I didn't hear her words. I felt them. "If you want to heal, just let go. It's time to let all the pain go. When you are ready, just simply step through to the other side," she said, gesturing toward a shimmering archway off in the distance.

I knew I had found my goal. I had my prize to focus on. It was the entryway back to that inner sanctum of my soul I had just experienced as a tourist, the place where I was full and whole and complete; the state of mind where I reintegrated and reclaimed back into me again all the lost parts of myself that right now were still archived in ice.

I knew at that moment I wasn't ready to walk through. I knew this experience was just the start, and that archway was marking the finish line. I still had work to do. I had those lost parts of myself that needed to be heard and witnessed so they could let their pain go. They needed to come out of the freeze and heal.

For that, I knew I needed time—and, as it turned out, mushrooms and weed.

PART 4

Shayla—The New Normal

CHAPTER 14

Just Say Yes

"Are you fixed yet?" Joe asked me flippantly one morning a few months after we'd arrived back home from our Mexico trip. We were in the bedroom, and I'd just stepped off the scale.

"Ha!" I said, rolling my eyes at him. "I wish!" I could see my weight starting to slowly creep back up from the pounds I'd lost due to my healthy ayahuasca preparation diet, and I knew the warning signs. While I was no longer depressed, I still hadn't managed to make any significant lasting shifts in the way I behaved.

I kept trying, but my guards were clearly still in place.

* * *

The difference in my mood and attitude before and after taking ayahuasca was incredible. I came back from my trip with a renewed sense of energy and determination to heal my life.

However, as much as I wanted the ayahuasca experience to be a quick fix, one-and-done resolution of all my issues, I knew it would be more of a slow unraveling rather than an instantaneous, flick-of-the-cape, magician's reveal of my hidden self. "Trust the process," I kept overhearing Joe say to his friends. The catch phrase of his beloved basketball team, the Philadelphia 76ers. I knew I had to be patient. Recovering from trauma was a process with inevitable setbacks, as well as progress, along the way.

I also knew if I was going to get to a point in my emotional growth where I could pass through that archway, I needed a whole new approach to life and the way I'd been thinking. What I was doing before just wasn't working. Even with all the therapy techniques I'd tried, I couldn't stop getting mired in the deeply worn groves my unconscious and circular, mind-fucking, negative thoughts had ceaselessly tracked through my head.

I needed a fresh approach—a new *direction*, as we call it in Co-Co. A new, positive thought I would use repeatedly to wire different neural pathways in my brain.

One phrase kept coming back to me repeatedly.

I already had my new mantra. I'd been saying it since I first listened to that self-healing part of me when I was trapped and helpless in the pit and looking for a way out.

I want to live!

That voice had been quiet and timid at first, hard to hear amidst the noise of all the self-recrimination, guilt, and shame. But as I rose higher in my pit, those other voices fell away, and this voice grew louder and louder.

After the ayahuasca, that voice was almost deafening in my head. *I want to live! I want to live! I want to live!*

But I needed to learn how. All this time I had been alive, sure, but I hadn't been *living*. I had been existing. Surviving. On autopilot, going through the motions, and successfully faking it through the day.

The next time Cherie and I caught up on a video chat, I

tried to describe to her what I had realized. "I didn't really *feel* anything. I wasn't *in* my body. I mean, that's how I've been most of my life, to be honest, but particularly since I moved to Seattle. I was mostly numb, checked out, and emotionally absent."

"That sounds awful!" she said.

"I mean, it wasn't *all* the time, thankfully! Not in those times when I was at parties or special occasions, with friends, or especially when things were good with Joe. But you know, in the buildup to my rock bottom moment in 2018, like, *most* of the time!"

With the help of Mother Aya, I glimpsed a future where I finally gave myself permission to really, fully live. And I mean LIVE! In an all caps and a ton of redundant exclamation marks kind of way. I knew I wanted to feel and have passions, interests, hobbies, friends, great sex, and incredible food. I wanted to take care of my body. I wanted to spend time with my loved ones, contribute back to society, and experience the usual things healthy people see and do.

These were not new desires for me or outside of my realm of experience. With the help of Co-Co and other therapies, I had felt and done most of these things before, many times in my life, even if sometimes it was just briefly. *Why then didn't I let myself now? Why did I constantly sabotage any progress I made?* I repeatedly asked myself those first few months in dismay.

It took me a while, but then I realized: Knowing I wanted to live was great and all, but there was still something blocking my way.

Even though the ayahuasca had somewhat turned the sound down, all those anxious voices in my head were still around, guarding those ice cells. Dire warnings and other limiting beliefs all screamed at me with terrified voices.

Those voices were the echoes of Dad's, still trying to warn me and, simultaneously, keep me small and in check.

* * *

My guards were the ones who demotivated or blocked me or generally got in my way. They patrolled the levels of my high security prison, keeping tabs on the cells, making sure there were no escapes. They hated it whenever I tried to release any part they thought put me at a high risk of getting in trouble. They shut me down, sabotaged and denied, or even sometimes outright lied to avoid me becoming my full self. They were persistent, and sometimes, not even subtle.

When at first I tried to step back into the me that was healthy, active, and fit, I was met with resistance every step of the way. Every night I came home from work, went upstairs to change my clothes to exercise, and thought, *I promised myself I'd work out today.*

From somewhere deep in the recess of my heart I'd hear a determined voice reply, "No. I don't want to."

But I will feel so much better if I exercise.

"No. I don't want to."

I would then talk sternly to myself in the mirror. *Shayla. Seriously. You know this is what you want.*

"No! I don't want to," was the even stronger reply.

I need to do yoga. It will help with my sore joints and flexibility, and I'll be stronger and fitter again. Or maybe I should start belly dancing or rowing. I'd love that too.

The guarding voice would then turn up the volume and say, "Remember how dangerous it was to have a slim, athletic body? How happy you were? How much attention you got? And then, do you remember how ashamed you felt when you got in trouble with Dad, and he accused you of being a slut for showing off your body and trying to attract guys? You don't want to feel like that again, *do you*?"

No. I don't want to, I'd think, instinctively collapsing my posture and hunching my shoulders forward to hide my breasts.

"Besides that, you always hurt yourself when you try to exercise. You're already in so much pain with the injuries you have now. You don't want to do anything to increase that. *Do you*?"

No. I don't want to, I'd think in reply, happy to latch onto the excellent excuse presented.

So rather than put on my workout clothes, I'd slip off my bra and get into my pajamas, go back downstairs to look for something to eat, and sit and watch TV instead.

* * *

The biggest lie the guards perpetuated was that I didn't deserve anything. Not love, respect, success, or passion. It was the cause of every single unhappy and dissatisfying area of my life and always had been.

Before my rock bottom moment, I spiraled downward into the morass of the pity pit because I truly believed it was what I deserved. While I was subsumed by shame, guilt, and sadness, I had an existential tug-of-war with myself. The spark of my spirit, the part of me that wanted and knew I deserved to *live* (passionately and vibrantly), was in constant and direct conflict with the part of me that just didn't.

The further down the pit I went, the stronger and more smothering the guards became, until my spark was almost extinguished. It's not that I really wanted to end my life. I wasn't quite there yet. But what I did do was to put my life on hold. I went on strike from truly living.

It was too hard, and too much, to be motivated and excited; to actually do anything to further or benefit my life, when that was in direct opposition of what I felt I deserved. *I don't deserve to be happy. I don't deserve to succeed.*

That's what I first learned growing up with Dad and then my guards led me to believe.

First with ayahuasca, and later with mushrooms and weed, I deactivated the anxiety defenses and found the knock-out pill that put those guards to sleep, so I could continue the healing process in peace.

Once I did that, I released and reclaimed the parts of me that had my own best interests at heart: the champions for my cause who knew I deserved better; the ones I severed off over the years, and especially when I descended so deep into the pit. They let me feel joy, energy, and drive to do and succeed. Finally, I had free access to revive them and heard them speak. And when I did, the message I heard loud and clear was, "Yes!"

* * *

Reflecting on it now, it feels like the ayahuasca showed me a string of shiny, luminescent lanterns guiding my way up and out of the darkness, shepherding me back up out of my pit toward the fresh air and light. I found my own exit-row floor lighting leading me where I needed to go. I didn't question. I simply followed the trail and said yes to anything that came my way.

The pandemic put me on pause somewhat, but in 2019, I was a yes-saying machine.

In April, I said yes to doing another personal growth course. It had some pearls of wisdom and gave me some emotional growth insights, but the best thing I got out of it was my good friend, Elizabeth.

On the morning of the third day, I saw her on my way to the bathroom and, for some reason, stopped to chat. She was about to bail from the course, and I ended up persuading her not to leave. We hit it off immediately, and later that day, we went to lunch together at a Sushi restaurant in Fremont. "There's this week-long regional Burning Man camp I go to, called Critical, that I think you might like. If you—"

"Yes!" I said, before she even finished her sentence. "Yes, I want to go!"

I'd heard about Burning Man before. I knew about the popular event in the Black Rock Desert in Nevada known as "The Big Burn" where people came together and created an intentional community around their own clearly defined set of principles. They outlined how to be thoughtful and kind human beings and defined things like inclusion, consent, accountability, and even a culture of gifting.

The idea of a regional (smaller and local to Seattle) event immediately resonated with me. These were the same types of people and principles I already knew and loved and saw in my Confest and Co-counseling communities. I knew this would be different in many ways, but I also knew, like in those other spaces, with these people, I would be safe.

*　*　*

I went to Critical that July, knowing next to no one and alone, as Joe didn't want to come with me. I said yes to camping with complete strangers, Nora and Rusty, who were total sweethearts and made me feel welcome straight away. They gave me a home base from which I could explore, and I met so many other awesome people every day. I said yes to everything there and walked around the entire time with a huge grin on my face.

Never once did I feel unsafe in any way. I met people (or "Burners," as members of this community are known) from all walks of life, dressed up and dressed down. Costumes and outfits of all descriptions seemed to be the way Burners celebrated their existence. Tassels, leather, fake fur, body paint, and lots and lots of LED lights abounded. I wandered into theme camps and art cars and stopped random people to chat. I saw camps all about music or fire-twirling and even a submarine that blew fire from its ports.

One camp was called Hot Noods and served amazing ramen until late. Another was FunCon, which was short for Fun Intended Consequences and they ran a bar and lots of game nights. Others made grilled cheese when you needed it the most late in the evenings, or bacon and Bloody Marys for recovery in the mornings. However, it wasn't all drinking and games. Some camps held workshops on personal growth topics or to learn a new skill. Others had places to interact with art installations or just chill.

Here were my people! My tribe and allies. Here was the community I'd been so desperately missing.

"Of course you did! The place is full of Jews and hippies!" joked my friend, Staci, at a post-Critical party. We talked about how I immediately felt at home there and could let my guard down. Throughout my life, the times when I was the happiest was when I was immersed in my communities; where I found my friends. And *friends = safe*.

Therefore, more friends equaled more safe. I didn't even have to meet them. I just felt happy knowing they were there. Friends of friends. People who knew people. If my dad taught me anything, having connections was the way to go. As a kid, he often only ate because someone in his community got his mother a job doing laundry or gave them food out of charity.

There is safety in numbers. Never be alone. Always gather allies for a rainy day. Dad drilled into my head. As a kid, I learned that lesson well and was always drawn to anyone outside the house; anyone with somewhere safe if I needed to escape.

I know I wouldn't have survived my childhood as well as I did without the sanctuary of Christine's place. Even though we fell out of touch for a long time after I moved out of home, she was there when I needed her the most. All through my life, having my communities and family has been what's saved me. Within the Burner community, I also found the creative, passionate, active people who were happily *doing*. They weren't *move, distract, do*-ing in the same way I had been. They were *dream, plan, do*-ing to put their ideas and projects in place. It lit me up from the inside to walk around and see that creativity at work. *This is what living looked like!* It was a further reminder of the good things in store for me if I continued following Mother Aya's well-lit path.

*   *   *

After Critical, I followed an even brighter string of glowing yeses: yes to more Burner activities and parties, gatherings, dinners, and happy hours. Each time I went, I made new friends and strengthened the connections I'd already made. Throughout the year, I said yes to changing teams at work and starting a new job with less stress when I got back from leave. Yes to more camping and summer fun. Even a yes to a creativity workshop which rekindled my desire to write.

Since then, every night I came home from work, went upstairs to change my clothes to exercise, and would think, *I promised myself I'd work out today.*

From somewhere deep in the recess of my heart, I'd hear a determined voice reply, "No. I don't want to."

Oh okay. Well, how about I just start small then? I won't even get sweaty. Just an easy five minutes on the rower. I didn't even wait for an answer or bother to get changed as I sat down and strapped in my feet and lifted the handle. After a few weeks of that, my guard didn't even bother protesting or notice when I started upping the intensity and duration.

Each yes underlined my desire and firmed my resolve to fully and passionately *live*! All those positive activities rejuvenated my soul and heart in a way I hadn't fully felt since arriving in Seattle and not since my mum had died. Within a few months of taking the ayahuasca, I realized I was no longer frozen, depressed, and hiding in the pit. It was also about the time when I started doing my solo-therapy sessions with weed.

They were where I said a big *yes!* to doing the work to find self-love and self-respect. Yes to learning I deserve happiness and, most importantly, finally a yes to letting go of my guilt and shame. My sessions were how I learned to get past my guards and trust the process.

CHAPTER 15

2020

_____

The way 2020 started for us in Seattle should have been a huge omen for what was coming. For the first time since I've been here, there was no New Year's Eve fireworks display from the Space Needle because of the weather.

I used to love watching fireworks, but now I hate them for the noise and sheer trauma it induces in people and nearby animals. But, at the time, I was excited. For the first time, Joe and I had a prime viewing spot on the rooftop at our friend's place in Queen Anne. We were right there, drinks in hand, gathered and ready. All happy and anticipatory, counting down the seconds, and then… nothing.

That night should've shown us 2020 was going to be a bust. The way 2019 tipped over into 2020 was the Doomsday Clock chiming midnight. It was when the world said, "Fuck you! You had a great 2019? You should have known better!" I have never experienced a year like 2020, and I hope to God that none of us ever do again. It started with the bushfires in Australia and only got worse from there. I watched helpless and in horror as a record forty-seven million acres of my homeland burned. Thirty-four people died along with over one billion animals. Thirty-five hundred homes and thousands of other buildings went up in flames. Even for a country used to annual fires this was a disaster.

After a brief trip to Australia at the end of February, I arrived back in Seattle on March 9 and went straight into the COVID pandemic lockdown. I was one of the lucky ones. I was able to work from home and, thankfully, had my usual income throughout 2020. From March through the end of May, I adapted to the new normal. I watched in horror with everyone else as the number of cases and deaths started to climb. I was stressed and anxious but overall doing okay, as thankfully no one I knew directly was infected. We followed the guidelines and wore masks and stayed at home. The dog helped Joe's and my sanity by keeping us distracted with his usual antics and got me out of the house for at least an hour of exercise every day.

I explored more and more of my neighborhood on those walks. I finally saw who lived in the houses around me and struck up socially distanced conversations. Ironically, I felt more connected to Seattle during 2020 than I had in the seven years prior.

Then May 29 hit, and the Black Lives Matter (BLM) protests over the death of George Floyd started happening all around the country. Suddenly all hell broke loose in my usually peaceful surroundings, and all my worst fears, all the things I'd only seen before in my newsfeed or in movies or on TV, became a reality.

There were peaceful protests that turned into violent riots the likes of which I had never before seen up close. People protesting against police brutality were brutally attacked by the police or their supporters and then arrested. I saw the misinformation and propaganda the media was spinning that directly contradicted what I saw happening on the actual streets.

White supremacists shot and killed people less than two miles from my house. A car rammed into a crowd. Flash bangs went off and sent the neighborhood dogs crazy. In Capitol Hill, where most of the action happened, toxic pepper spray drove people from their homes, especially my friends with their new baby.

I heard the sirens constantly. I abided by the sudden curfew. I kept my head down as best I could while trying to support the cause and publicly stand up for what was right. I lived with a Black man—the very people they were targeting. There was no more hiding.

I was trapped. I couldn't run or go anywhere because of COVID. I couldn't go home to Australia even if I had wanted to; their borders were shut tight.

Even if I could have gone home, I'm not sure I would have felt any safer. Sure, they had effective lockdowns, which meant the pandemic wasn't such an issue, but there were still issues with racism. Anti-semitism and far-right ideology have been on the rise there for a while now. There was even a far-right demonstration with people doing Sieg Heils in St. Kilda. In Melbourne.

My Melbourne.

The safe haven my father left all he knew and loved behind for. The place meant to be as far away from fascists and nazis as he could get. The place I had grown up in and thought was safe.

I shouldn't have been surprised. I should have been prepared. I should have remembered I was lulled into a false sense of security in my beloved dinky-die, true-blue, Aussie upbringing. I believed it was different there. I was so tightly wrapped up in my little privilege bubble that I didn't see or want to care.

I told Joe when we were preparing for a special podcast

episode in June on the BLM and George Floyd events, "I didn't really look at how, as a nation, Australians treated our indigenous people and immigrants. I didn't want to recognize that it was the same people who colonized and terrorized the indigenous people here, who did exactly the same to the aborigines back home." We had a literal White Australia policy up until 1966, and it took us until 1962 before Aboriginal and Torres Strait Islander people were allowed to vote. They weren't even required to enroll and participate in elections like the rest of Australians until 1984.

Living with Joe opened my eyes to racism in a way I couldn't unsee. Before I moved here, I had been so busy hiding my head in the sand that it took me until then to really understand. All the things I was scared of happening to me were already happening all around the world daily. They always had been—2020 just removed the screen.

However, as hard as 2020 was, it is an absolute testimony to how far I'd come already by that stage that I didn't just implode. I recently told my friend Kathryn over video chat, "If 2020 would have happened in 2018 or even in early 2019, I wouldn't have stood a chance. "Back then I was running on fumes. I was so emotionally maxed out. I had nothing left in the tank. But thank God I did the ayahuasca when I did. I think it literally saved my life, or at least my sanity. It shored up my battery. Without all the yeses of 2019, I would not have been able to handle 2020!" Don't get me wrong. During most of 2020, even though I wasn't in my misery pit and frozen, my anxiety turned up to pre-ayahuasca levels. It almost consumed me, and despite how far out I'd come, it almost threw me back down again.

But it didn't. Because thank all the gods, I had weed! I would *not* have survived 2020 without it. In Seattle, the dispensaries stayed open during the pandemic. Essential services indeed! It was what made the pandemic, for me, not just bearable but, surprisingly, incredibly productive.

*   *   *

The greatest gift and biggest surprise of me taking weed was it not only brought me into the present, but it helped me feel safe enough to stay there. It put me in suspended animation in the pause between my thoughts and heartbeats. It gave me what I'd always sought but didn't know how to achieve.

Peace.

Silence in my head.

It shushed my father's ever-present commands and criticisms. It turned down the volume on my erratic, manic, doomsday-prophetic, high-pitched, terrorized thoughts that played on a never-ending loop inside my brain. It gave my frazzled, burned out, and over-taxed nervous system what it needed to recover.

Time and quiet.

*   *   *

One evening in late August in 2020, Joe and I were on the rooftop of our townhouse. The sun was slowly setting, and magic hour light draped the landscape in liquid gold. Joe was grilling on the barbecue, and the air smelled delicious and fragrant. I was sitting at a little cast-iron table, reading. Our dog, tired of running back and forth snapping at bugs, was panting at my feet.

Joe started playing music on his phone, so I stood up, wrapped my arms around his waist, put my head against his chest, and we began slow-dancing.

It was cozy, romantic, and sweet.

It couldn't have been more different than literally hours before, when we were at each other's throats and was in stark contrast to how I felt in that moment. I didn't know why my emotions shifted so radically in such a short time, and seemingly for no reason, but then it dawned on me: I'd taken an edible and was just now feeling its effects. It calmed me down.

Suddenly I could tell the distinct difference in how I thought and acted when I was anxious to how I felt and behaved when I was high.

After doing the ayahuasca, taking an edible and getting high (once I got the dosage right) was a completely different experience. I finally clapped my hands, said, "I believe," and let the magic happen.

Weed taught me the palpable difference between when I was anxious and stuck in sympathetic mode and when I dropped into the parasympathetic. It helped me chill the fuck out. I now had a vignette filter around my world, dimming out the unhelpful, toxic, and damaging thoughts and bringing into light-filled focus the good, helpful, and healing ones.

Finally, the constant background buzz drowning out all my trapped positive inner voices was muted. I heard with crystal clarity for the first time in my life exactly what my exiled parts of self were trying to tell me. Up until then, they were muffled by the angry white noise of all my negativity; my worry and terror at living.

This shouldn't have been a surprise in any shape or form as I'd been using weed for a while now, but this was the first time it reached my conscious awareness of what it somatically felt like to be calm and present. It was a revelation. Once I consciously tuned into the feeling, I found I could recreate it without the weed. It resuscitated my emotional muscle memory, and I could go back to that feeling any time I wanted, even if it was just briefly.

Logically I should have always known I was anxious. It's so clear in hindsight, but it was a "forest and trees" kind of situation.

"I get anxious!" I exclaimed softly to Joe with the dawning awareness. I pulled away from his embrace to look up at him as we danced. "That's why I fight and get so defensive."

"You're joking, right?" he responded with a grimace.

This was not news to him. Clearly this was something he knew from the outset, but it was new to me.

⋏   ⋏   ⋏

However, despite my best efforts, 2020 severely tested my limits. Joe and I had a conversation around my lingering anxiety some time toward the end of the year.

"I think about all these dystopian things happening every day. *Every. Day,*" I told Joe one night on the couch.

"All these different ways that something bad is going to happen to you, me, the puppy, Seattle, or my family. I'm constantly worried about everyone I love *all* the time, and it's exhausting."

"I would suggest you stop doing that," Joe responded seriously.

"I *want* to stop doing that, but I don't know how! I constantly feel unsafe."

"The world *is* unsafe. Bad things happen. But if they're gonna happen, they're gonna happen. If they don't, they're not. Worrying about bad things happening all the time doesn't allow you to, like, live," Joe said earnestly, giving me his full attention.

"I know, Joe. I know! That's exactly why my mantra

since doing ayahuasca is I want to *live*! I *want* to fucking live! I'm tired of being swamped by this heavy weight of fear. It's been holding me down from fully living for most of my life. That's why I keep telling you I'm having these profound experiences, and they're profound because I've never had these insights before.

"I could never see that there's a different choice to take; a different way of being, or thinking, and... it's helping." "I'm glad to hear that. If it helps more, think about it this way: What are the actual chances all these bad things are gonna happen to you or those you know? Because the odds are small in the grand scheme of things. Compared to the rest of the population or the geographical region we're in, we are not taking unnecessary risks. We aren't out in gangs or on a frontline in some war-torn country, and probably more relevant to our real situation right now, when we're around other people, we wear masks, or stay home and keep our head down. There are a ton of people like us who end up just dying of old age."

What he said made a lot of sense and helped me feel better. I've been working on it every day since, and while there are still some residual voices in my head, now they are so faint they are barely discernible.

Don't relax. Don't let your guard down. Happy isn't allowed to last, they whisper.

And I want to pummel those voices into the ground. I am so sick and tired of hearing them. So freaking tired of giving them air time. *It does not serve me*, I remind myself whenever I hear them now.

Despite my efforts, they still try to hold me back. Hold me down. They try to keep me small and powerless and in victim mode *all the time*! I don't want to feel like that. Being scared all the time is not living. It's existing. It's surviving.

And I'm tired of it. I can't control what happens in the future—I can only control my here and now. So, that's what I do. In this moment, in the present, I can be happy for as long as I want. Moment by moment.

And without weed, doing what all those years of meditations and therapy could not, I would never have found that out.

CHAPTER 16

Session Work

———

The most disruptive thing that happened for me in 2020 however, wasn't the turbulence or political and social upheaval going on around me, it was the quiet revolution going on inside my bathroom and heart. 2019 was when I started my healing sessions, but 2020 was when they got going in earnest. Thanks to the pandemic and being shut in, I suddenly had no social activities to distract me. I finally had much-needed time on my hands, and lots of it. It was hard before the pandemic, but then it became almost impossible to find a therapist, so I started self-medicating with edibles and doing my own version of self-help. I called these little moments of THC-induced self-reflection, emotional release, and healing, "sessions," as if I was having a Co-Co session, but with myself in the role of both the counselor and client.

To be totally clear, *this was not standard Co-Co practice, as there are no intoxicants allowed at all, for either party, in one of their sessions.* But I did beg, borrow, and steal mercilessly from the Co-Co toolkit of techniques and training, along with every other healing modality I'd ever learned. I did roleplay, mirror work, yoga, positive thinking, compassion, mindfulness, gratitude, and inner-child work. I asked myself, "What's that thought?" "What's the worst that could happen?" "What do you want to say right now?" All the amazing questions and tools I learned to help me dive deeper. The ones I used the most often, and now thanks to weed, I had access to answers for were: "Where is it in your body?" and "How do you feel?" I also repeatedly gave myself the instruction, "Breathe!"

When I needed it, I had an unconventional co-counselor who kept me safe by having part of my attention in the present: my dog, Yuengling (pronounced *Ying*-Ling, or just Yueng for short). He is a German shepherd-boxer cross, who was four at the time and gave me excellent, aware, caring attention. I should also mention at this point that yes, he is named after Joe's favorite Philly beer. It was a bargaining chip I used to get Joe to come around to the idea of getting a dog, as he didn't want one when I first broached the subject.

When I was in a session Yueng would come in and give me grounding touch by putting his head on my knee whenever he heard my breathing change or I started cry-ing. He tried to climb into my lap and lick my face if he thought I was too distressed. If I was lost down a rabbit hole of self-reflection for too long, he sat on my feet or scooted his butt in between my legs, demanding a back rub. I always knew he was close by, giving me unconditional love and no judgment whenever I looked into his eyes. He was *the best* at keeping things confidential, and I can't tell you the amount of times he's just sat there as I've hugged him and sobbed into his neck. For his "session time," I'd return the favor by taking him for a walk or playing fetch.

*   *   *

Around April 2020, Friday nights became "session nights." I took my edible and told Joe (if he was home), "I'm going upstairs to do a session." It was my signal that I didn't want to be disturbed and I'd be gone for a few hours. I'd go up to the bedroom or down to my study, close the door, and once the dog was settled, I'd tune out the rest of the world and tune into myself.

This was when the most incredible things started to happen. As I was doing it at home, by myself, on my own schedule, I dealt with my issues as they came up, in the moment I felt triggered. I didn't have to sit in therapy some time later and remember what bothered me and try to recreate my reaction. I was living and dealing with it in real time. I fully recognize I would not have been able to do that without years of Co-Co training and practice. I imagine that most people would benefit from a therapist or at least a trip sitter being present.

Every day, seemingly insignificant moments suddenly presented the greatest of gifts to me. They gave me crystal clear examples of what bothered me and what I was ignoring. I could see it now. I could hear those inner voices. I learned how to react, not from a place of a scared little child or a rebellious teenager or a humiliated young woman—I learned how to react to my life now as the integrated Shayla. I learned how to listen to Michelle, Mitch, and even little Misha.

* * *

Each session was different. Sometimes I deliberately started by asking the Co-Co question, "What's on top?" Was something urgent and pressing that needed my immediate attention? But that didn't happen often. Usually, I listened to music or a meditation, watched TV, or just talked to Joe.

Something I saw or heard triggered me, and I'd be off down a path of inner contemplation.

I'd often end up doing an unprompted session in the bathroom, as I'd go to wash my hands and catch sight of myself in the mirror. I don't know if you've ever *really* looked at yourself when you're high, but I recommend it.

*　*　*

"Are you okay in there?" Joe called to me one night. I'd been gone for almost an hour. One of the negative side effects of doing sessions when I'm high is I lose my sense of time and, sometimes, the thread of the conversation.

I stood there, trapped in a trance, looking at myself as if I saw my face and body for the first time. It was a revelation to me to be that present and in my body and not dissociated. It was like I saw the world, and my place in it, from a whole new perspective.

From that vantage point, I spontaneously started doing my mirror work, addressing my reflection as if it was the part I was trying to free. I simply had a conversation with myself, with my reflection answering completely honestly.

"Hello, you!" I said to my reflection. "What do you need? What can I do for you to help you feel complete?" Then I stood there and gave myself loving eye contact.

As I stared at them, my eyes in the mirror welled up. I felt those tears to be from when I was young and scared; maybe around the time just after the closet incident or a few years later. Either way, she started to tremble and then cried.

I stood in the bathroom and wrapped my arms tight around my shoulders, holding myself in a hug.

"It's okay. Just let it out. I know you were scared," I said soothingly to my reflection while I reached around and slowly stroked my own shoulders. I spoke as my present forty-nine-year-old self. "It was awful what you went through."

"I was all alone!" she sobbed back at me. "No one came to help me."

"I've got you. I've got you. You're not alone now," I responded soothingly, continuing to hold myself in a tight hug. "I'm so proud of you. You were so brave. You did what you needed to do to keep us safe. Thank you!"

After a few moments, the sobbing stopped and I let my arms hang down. The peak of THC-induced emotion started to recede. It had done its work. My inner child was heard and could now come out of hiding in the closet—and the freeze.

* * *

To help a part be released, I let them direct me and take over my body. I let them have access to what I'd denied them for so long. I let them *feel*. I let them cry or dance or move or shake or scream. Whatever they want and whatever it takes to get the emotional clearing.

I later learned from Dr. Aimie that by stretching the muscles, you are also stretching the nervous system and helping it to release. But at that stage, I'd been doing it instinctively. I experimented with stretching in ways I hadn't for a long time. Breathing deep into each move, I gently moved into my joints and did yoga poses or belly dancing shimmies.

Joe thought I was insane as I slow-danced my way through the house. I'd jog laps around the kitchen island or do ballet in the hallway. I did arabesques off the stairs and slow yoga, kickboxing, or rowing. Sometimes I curled into a ball on my bed and wept; whatever my high body told me to do. It helped me beyond belief. I reconnected that somatic feeling with the corresponding emotion, and that's what led directly to the healing.

After the session, I'd have to rest.

"You done crying yet?" was always Joe's question.

I was, but I was also happier, fuller; a more complete person. One more piece of my fractured core was restored again, allowing me access to more aspects of myself. Depending on the part I'd freed, I could now even without the weed, be cheeky or flirty, smart or creative any time I chose. I could select an emotional response at will. I could literally feel that part somatically, like I was stepping into a full-body sensory costume.

Joy returned to my chest and excitement in my belly; pain in my sternum when I thought of loss and grief. But this time, the bad feelings didn't last long or linger. I felt them, and then they passed. After being on high alert and keeping that part in the freeze state for all that time, my whole nervous system finally released the body to the long-awaited parasympathetic mode, and I breathed a spontaneous sigh of relief.

Before my weed sessions, I didn't realize how much I held my breath or how shallow I was breathing. It was like a break of sunshine through the rain. My soul suddenly breathed again. *I* could breathe again; stretch and move and *feel*! It gave me back my feeling, my sensations. I was present. I was embodied instead of drifting off somewhere else, completely dissociated.

"I feel like I'm brilliant when I'm high. I have confidence. My posture is straighter and taller. I think more creatively. I am definitely funnier. I'm a *much* better writer. And I can talk to you in a way I never could before," I declared to Joe one night after a session as we sat on the couch watching a movie. "Not only that, but for the first time in my life, I'm giving myself permission to think and feel. And to heal."

"That's great, babe," he replied, only giving me half of his attention. He was used to these proclamations by now.

I became curious again and motivated to learn. I started reading more about how this worked. I found YouTube videos like the one from Simeon Keremedchiev's TEDx Talk, called "Psychedelics: Effects on the Human Brain and Physiology," that explained the effects of plant medicine on the brain. I learned more about the way psychedelics help the nerve cells in the brain (neurons) grow and increase the complexity of their connections and pathways. It told me what I already knew: the ayahuasca had literally given my mind the ability to think differently.

Then, once I used the weed to tone down my negative thoughts and anxiety, (while it naturally turned up my empathy), I found the more often I repeated a new thought, like *I am safe* or *I deserve*, or even *I want to live*, the harder it stuck. I was strengthening the neural connections making the thought possible, so each time I repeated it to myself, I hardwired positive thoughts of self-love into the chemistry of my brain.

*   *   *

Around May of 2020, I took an edible and went to bed thinking I'd do a session. Lying there half in and half out of the covers, I restlessly tossed and thrashed around as I couldn't get physically comfortable. I had taken it too late in the evening. It was now past 1:00 a.m., and my brain would not shut off nor my body settle. I should have known better. I knew what was coming, so I lay back and let it.

The surge of feeling gathered momentum in my chest. I

waited first for the crescendo of loss, guilt, and shame forcing its way out of my body, catching a wave on torrents of tears. Next would be the logical connections and the insights freed by the physical catharsis that would inevitably follow.

This time, however, instead of the usual sadness, the emotion that welled up and exploded out of me like a wave shooting out of a blow hole was anger. It was palpable and seemed fathomless in its depths.

Growing up, anger was dangerous. Anger was forbidden. Anyone's anger apart from Dad's, that is.

And Dad was so, so angry. He didn't have a safe, healthy outlet for that anger, so he just dumped it all onto us. He had free reign to express his anger; his wrath, his indignation, annoyance, and irritation. He had every right to be angry, but we also had every right to not be the focus of it.

So I learned to suppress my anger. I shoved it deep, deep down inside my belly where I piled food on top to keep it there. All my life I'd smothered my anger, but in that moment, I felt it all. It came out white-hot and molten. I seethed in rage and indignation.

Anger at my father for treating all of us the way he did.

Anger at the world, and the people in it, for being so cruel and unkind.

Anger at myself for wasting so much of my own time not truly living.

But mostly, I was angry at my mother.

I wanted to ask her these questions all my life, but I missed my chance, so I raged at her instead inside my mind.

Why didn't you protect me? Why did you ignore me as an infant when I needed you the most? Why did you push me away when I tried to seek comfort from you? Why did you let him hit us, yell at us, dominate and control us, terrify us? Why did you put up with it? Put up with his abusive language and violent outbursts? Why didn't you take us away and put safety of distance between us and him?

Clearly she couldn't respond, and I can't say for sure, but knowing what I do about my own response to trauma, once I calmed down, I could guess the answer.

She was frozen too, I realized with tears in my eyes.

She, like me, equally loved and was terrified by him. She knew he needed help. She knew underneath all the bluff and anger he was fragile.

She was also, like me, loyal.

He'd lost so much, and she knew he couldn't lose us too. Knowing that didn't help her stand up to him—it didn't help her fight back. She withdrew instead. She's how I learned to check out. She's how I learned to be passive aggressive and put up with shit.

She was no match for my dad's grief and anger. She was so young when she married him. I don't think she felt strong enough to leave or safe enough to effectively intercept when he raged. Now I know, for her, just like with my dad, she did the best she could with the resources she had. I don't know exactly what went through her mind or what they said behind closed doors, but I do know when I was very young, she was in the bottom of her own misery pit, trapped, depressed, and scared. If that wasn't enough, she also went through early menopause and had her own health issues.

You were far away from your home and had few friends. You were doing what you could when you could do it. I acknowledged her silently in my mind.

The rest of the time, like the rest of us, she just tried to survive.

CHAPTER 17

Be Seen, Be Heard

One morning, in the beginning of May 2019, Joe and I were doing our usual stay-in-bed-until-the-last-possible-moment thing before finally getting up to go to work. Yueng was in his pride of place, snuggled between Joe's legs with his head using Joe's foot as a pillow. We were both on our phones. I was catching up on emails and Joe was watching something on YouTube.

"Hey, babe!" he said, turning to me all excited and enthusiastic. "Let's do a podcast!"

The minute Joe saw the trailer for the new Damon Lindelof TV show, *Watchmen*, he knew he wanted to do a podcast on it.

The minute I watched it, I equally knew I did not.

I knew the show would be about the things I didn't want to think about, let alone share those thoughts with the world. Racial discrimination, police brutality, and white supremacy. The fact that it was a superhero comic book story was beside the point, and I told him as much.

"Come on. I need someone to talk to. I can't do it on my own," Joe said when I politely said nope to his offer to be his co-host.

My gut clenched, and warning bells went off in my head at the thought of publicly discussing those topics: coming out against authority. Defending the minority. Having an opinion— especially one not necessarily in alignment with the current political administration's views and policies on these issues.

This deeply distressed me. It meant being heard and seen.

I explained to him my immediate fear, that of stirring the pot and making ourselves a target for recrimination or reprisal. I knew exactly how contentious these topics were and how much of a hot button we would be pushing, and this was even before the events of 2020!

This was the exact opposite of everything I had spent my life doing. This was the *opposite* of hiding.

"We can use vigilante names if that makes you feel any better," he said, somewhat conceding to my concerns.

Surprisingly, the promise of anonymity did make me feel better, or, at any rate, more willing to try it.

Adding to my apprehension about being thrust into the spotlight, I also worried I wouldn't have anything of value to add to this conversation, because 1) I'm not Black, and 2) I hadn't seen the movie or read the comics.

Joe reminded me that both weren't an issue, and by the time the show started in October that year, I was prepared with background on the characters, along with the comic book and movie canon; however, I was still vastly unprepared emotionally for the level of raw vulnerability our podcast required. Season one, episode one: "It's Summer and We're Running Out of Ice." The opening scene was of a fucking *literal* massacre. The 1921 Tulsa Massacre. That really happened. Not fiction. Not fantasy. A real-life massacre of real Black people who, up until that point, peacefully, prosperously, and *happily* went about their own business.

Right out of the gate, I saw my greatest fears played out.

Happy wasn't allowed to last. The. World. Is. Not. Safe.

I saw in my mind's eye the beginning of every Holocaust movie I'd ever watched. The part where they are living their lives and having their Friday night Shabbat dinners before the door gets kicked in by jackboots.

Suddenly, I saw with crystal clarity the similarity between Joe and my father.

I understood why the thought of this had chilled me to the bone; the reason why every time Joe left the house to do even a simple errand, I was worried he was never going to make it home.

I feared for his safety every time he wasn't in my sight, whether at work or going to the supermarket. Every single thing I'd seen and heard since being in the USA and living with Joe was how much more of a risk and *reality* it was that Joe, as a Black man, could be shot, arrested, or violently assaulted. Things my father told me could happen to me, because they had happened to him—could quite likely happen to Joe.

My dad was denigrated, persecuted, and discriminated against in the worst possible way. He was treated as less than human, disposable, insignificant, and inferior.

Every. Single. Day. I saw the same things happen in this country and around the globe to minorities and immigrants; to people of all persuasions, to those who did not meet the "right" criteria set by the people in power.

*   *   *

I never listened to the news or read the paper as a kid. I still avoid it now. I didn't want to know that everything my dad warned me about was happening. I didn't want to hear or see it for the same reason I didn't want to read my dad's book—because then it would be real; to people I knew and loved, in the here and now. It also meant those bad things could happen to me too.

But Joe likes to stay informed, and he equally likes to share bad news with me. It was my dad speaking with Joe's voice as the harbinger of doom. So now I have a rule with Joe: no news before midday.

"No, Joe!" I reminded him one morning late in 2020. "No more showing me another news item about a Black man being killed by police, or lynched in a tree, or shot while out jogging. No reddit posts of toddlers being stolen from their mothers for a photo opportunity or a Black woman shot while home. In her bed. *Asleep!* I need to function. I need to have at least the illusion for a few hours that I am safe. That you are safe. That there is peace."

I just couldn't wake up to another Black child murdered for walking down the street or a Black mentally-incapacitated man gunned down because he couldn't speak. I couldn't hear about Asians being spat at on the street and school, mosque, synagogue, or other mass shootings.

It's not that I didn't care. It's that I cared too much. It hit too close to home.

Every door I saw kicked in with military style boots, every story of cops being let off for *literal* murder, every time I saw one of those news stories, I heard my father.

"Bad things happen to good people. The world is not kind.

The world is full of hate. The. World. Is. Not. Safe!"

Every single day, I saw and heard hate. So, so much hate.

People hated because of their skin. Because of their language. Because of their religion or their sexual or political orientation. There was no escape. It was on my Facebook page, in Instagram comments, in Reddit posts, and of course, on the news. It was in movies and on TV and campaign posters too.

* * *

My father always warned me, "You know World War III is coming. You know peace won't last. And you know how much the world hates Jews. Don't let them know who you are. Don't let them have that power over you. *Blend in. Hide. Don't stand out.* Your gift is in your normalcy. Don't be too good or bad. Don't be too pretty or too ugly, too happy or sad. Stay small. Stay hidden. Stay safe. Stay alive."

So I hid. All my life I hid who I was. What I am. I hid my religion and my heritage and my identity. The fact that I am Jewish is one of the last things people used to find out about me. But now, I have a digital yellow star I can't take off. It's superimposed over me as a holographic heads-up display. Wherever I go, at home, to work, or just down the street, it follows me into this real world and shatters my illusion that I have a cloak of invisibility around me.

I don't know who's digitally watching, listening, or keeping track. I feel exposed and violated. It's something I didn't fully buy into, even though I said "I agree" to every user agreement and cookie. I know there is nothing I can do about it now except live off the grid, but that is counter to everything that nourishes me. It is so hard to stay in contact with friends and family without technology.

* * *

For a few months, Joe kept asking if I wanted to do the podcast with him, and I kept feeling my resistance. I knew I needed a session. I knew I needed to let go of this fear. I knew it stunted my growth and held me back from truly living. I also knew I loved Joe and wanted to share what I had seen and experienced; how obvious it was that Black lives mattered. It wasn't even a question.

I took an edible one Friday night and sat on the edge of the bath in our upstairs bathroom. I stretched into the constriction in my shoulders and neck, then stood and circled my knees and heard them creak and release.

Then I let the weed do its magic as I tried to relax and tune into me.

I thought about what was under the surface and triggering me about doing the podcast and talking about things that really mattered. I thought about which part of me was locked away and what they had been trying all this time to say.

But my inner voice was stunted. Halted. Cut off and small. I couldn't complete a full thought to its conclusion. It was blocked, like I had hit a wall and I couldn't follow the trail anymore. I had hit a dead zone and was not receiving the signal. All I got was white noise and nothingness when I tried to take my thoughts in that direction.

When that happened, I knew I'd run into a guard. It was a white-out blizzard I couldn't pass. I knew my brain was protecting me. I needed to find another path, down, around, over—whatever I needed to do to avoid the roadblock and keep pushing through.

"Shayla. Breathe. Just stop and breathe," I said out loud, waiting for the weed to let my guard down.

I know what to do. I just can't seem to let myself do it! I cried in earnest at this thought as I finally felt the helplessness.

I've listened to lectures on self-esteem and read every Brené Brown book on the need to seize the day, be vulnerable, know my own power, and speak my truth. I know *what I need to do,* I thought as I stood up and looked myself directly in the mirror, fully challenging my current self to take responsibility. *But if I live my perfect life, if I let myself be fully in my power and let all the parts of me step fully into the light... I am betraying my dad.* I started sobbing again as the insight dawned on me what the real misbelief was that powered me for all these years and who the part was I'd locked away.

That scared little girl inside of me, not wanting to do anything to anger or disappoint her daddy, was guarded by the negative voice pounding my confidence and self-esteem. It had been telling me, *Forget about doing the podcast. Stay where it is safe. Stay hidden. Stay mundane. Stay untalented and unnoticed. It's safer that way.*

My guard tried to make me believe that by sticking to Dad's rules of not standing out, not being happy, or truly living for me, that somehow I'd keep myself safe. But all I did was keep myself small, weak, and waste the life I'd been given. I repressed my strength, joy, love, and power, so I never realized my true, full potential. The part locked away inside the cell spoke to me.

She said, "You put me here because you thought I needed to be hidden from the world. You thought they needed to be Jedi mind-tricked so they would pass on by. You wanted to let me fade into the background and into obscurity."

It's true. I believed I had to shove deep down inside who I really was because showing the true me was dangerous. Mortally dangerous. Deep, deep, deep down inside I felt hunted. I was forever being stalked and pursued and targeted. There was a constant fucking bullseye on my back just below the surface, and only if I kept it well-hidden would I be okay.

If they see me, they can hurt me = I am not safe.

I let out my breath.

I am not safe. The quintessential *I.*

The habits, traits, thoughts, behaviors, beliefs, and opinions making up who a person really is as an individual—their *I.*

My *I* was not safe and never had been. It had never been safe for me to speak up or out or to say what I really wanted or felt. Only what Dad wanted mattered.

You can do anything you want to do, as long as it's what I want you to do came back to haunt me.

So I didn't speak up. I didn't have a passion for any cause. I didn't take any action because action-takers were safe in their *I.* Safe to their core that they had a right to stand up and be seen, be heard, and be exposed. I didn't feel I had that right—or should I say, privilege— because unfortunately, it is a privilege for a few when it should be a right for everyone.

Instead, I sat back and tried to stuff my passion and feelings down so they didn't crack my carefully curated façade. I couldn't show anyone how I truly felt about cops murdering Black people in their beds, or in their schools, or defenseless face-down on the pavement. I couldn't show my rage and terror at their situation in public because that would put a target on me too. I couldn't step into the spotlight and call out the perpetrators, because that spotlight, the threat of being persecuted, was precisely what I was hiding from.

As my breathing slowed back to normal, I knew what I had to do. I couldn't keep running and hiding my whole life from what is in my DNA.

Even if I keep my head down, when the shit hits the fan, there are already digital records of who I am. I can't pass for a local the way my dad did. I can no longer hide in plain sight and blend in. That ship has sailed. I don't have hacker connections who can magically erase my digital footprint if necessary. It's all out there for anyone to see. No matter how concerned I am about my privacy or security, that cat is out of the bag now. There is no more hiding that I am an immigrant and a minority. I knew it was time I stepped out of the shadows. Joe couldn't hide in plain sight. His Blackness went with him everywhere. I needed to own who I was and stop denying I was different. I needed to stop trying to blend in. I wasn't much of an ally if I stayed safely hidden.

I decided to learn the lesson technology was teaching and let go of any pretense that I wouldn't be seen. I embraced the parts of me begging to be released.

I said, "Fuck it. I'm in," to doing the *Watchmen* podcast. I knew full well what the repercussions could be and exposed my soft underbelly to anyone who chose to download and listen.

* * *

As I watched the *Watchmen* episodes, my amazement grew. I was so impressed with the writing and subtext and the clear messages Lindelof was getting across. Maybe he saw the world the same way I did. Maybe he saw that it didn't matter who wore the uniform and who was targeted—the hatred was still the same. It hadn't gone away at the end of the war; it just went underground.

Oh! I thought with recognition and a touch of relief as Joe and I got into the podcast and dissected the show and its themes. *This is about trauma! Intergenerational trauma. This I understand. This I can talk about.*

In one episode of our podcast, I came out of the

proverbial closet, put myself out there, and announced to the world I was Jewish, because I want to fully live, and I couldn't do that if I was still hiding.

I want to be heard. I want to be seen. I want to be fully me.

CHAPTER 18

I Love You, Puppy

———

When is it my turn? I'd think whenever I went to one of the (fifty-six and counting) weddings I'd been to in my life so far.

When am I going to have the wedding and the house and the husband and the dog and the kids?

I desperately wanted the craftsman house with the double garage and white picket fence in the cool, leafy inner-city neighborhood. I wanted the life I saw, and was led to want, by romance novels and happy TV sitcoms. I had this idea that when I got all that, my life would be perfect. That's when I could finally start living the life I was meant to have and be the person I was meant to be. The time when I wasn't betraying my dad by being happy; living normally, independently. Living *for me.*

Of course, even though I already had a house and a man and a dog, all of which I love and who love me, I still wasn't letting myself be happy. I was still waiting for my turn; waiting for Dad's permission or blessing to have a safe home and my own family.

* * *

One evening a few months ago, I took an edible and did a session while Joe was at work. The edible kicked in, and I was in the stimulus phase of the session where anything would trigger me and send me off down the rabbit hole of self-exploration.

Yueng, my constant delight and source of joy, was curled up on his bed by the living room window, looking effortlessly adorable. I don't know how he manages to make himself into such a small ball of fur sometimes, yet other times, stretch out to take up the entire bottom of a king-sized bed.

I looked at him, and as usual, a warm gooey gush of love seeped into my heart. *I fucking love you, puppy!* I thought as my eyes rested on him, drinking him in. It wasn't just his floppy boxer ears and German shepherd soft black and tan fur and smoky eyes that made me love him so much—it was all of it. It was his sharp intelligence and stubbornness, his playfulness, and his willingness to let me smother him in kisses and rub his silky belly.

I could go on all day about the cute things he does, and don't even get me started on how endearing it is when the fire engine goes by and he howls his fraternal answering call to its wailing siren.

I snap into John Wick mode the instant I think anything or anyone will hurt him. I want to protect him with my life when I look into his eyes and see his innocent love and trust staring back at me.

I realized I did what I always did whenever I looked at him: I stopped time and stepped into the present moment to love and adore him and savor every minute with my baby.

At the thought of him as my baby, my eyes instantly welled up and my throat constricted. Something about that hit a nerve. As I moved to the bathroom, I knew the answer by the time I got into the room and shut the door.

By adopting Yueng, I directed all the affection I'd stored up over the years to give to a baby and child onto him instead.

He gave me an outlet for that nurturing, maternal love I had nowhere else to express. I got to take care of him and look out for him in a way I couldn't do to anyone else.

I finally opened the cell door and listened to the part of me going through perimenopause, the most recent part of me suddenly grieving the freshly realized loss of any future opportunity for me to have my own children.

The pain was raw and primal. I sobbed deeply and let it wash over me.

I was only a few minutes into this emotional release when I heard Joe, concerned, call out to me from the kitchen. "Are you okay? Are you crying?"

By this stage, Joe had come home and heard me in the bathroom.

"Yes. Yes. I'm fine. I'm just having a moment," I replied through the door as I quickly wiped my nose and washed my face. I pulled myself together enough to go out and sit with him on the couch.

"What was all that about? Why do all your moments have to involve crying?" he asked.

"I was crying because I was feeling grief about not having kids."

"Where did that come from?" He was confused and caught off guard.

I explained about looking at Yueng and how it triggered me. "I was crying to release the grief that we aren't having kids. That it never happened for us," I replied, my eyes starting to water again as soon as I said those words out loud.

Yueng heard my voice and breathing change and came to put his head on my knee. He then scrambled to get on to the couch and into my lap.

"But I never pushed it. I never said we're done if we don't have kids. I never wanted to go to a fertility clinic or even to an adoption agency," I said as I started stroking the top of Yueng's head.

"But you could have had kids before you met me if you really wanted them," Joe pointed out, somewhat defensively, as if I had accused him of stopping me.

"Yes. You are right. I could have. That's the grief!" I said, my voice catching again. "I never let myself *want* to have kids. "I never felt it was *okay* to have kids. To have a family of my own. I was always so scared I'd raise them the way I was raised. I'd fuck them up. And then once Mum died, I was so scared I'd have them and lose them too."

Joe sat there and listened. "Right," he said simply, acknowledging my pain.

After a few moments of sitting together with tears rolling down my cheeks, washing away the grief, he got up to go to the kitchen to make dinner. "But I'm taking away your weed. It makes you cry too much!" he joked, breaking the tension and making me laugh.

* * *

I am so proud to be a parent to that dog. I feel so bad we stole him away from his pack, his kind. We neutered him so he couldn't have any offspring of his own and then made him abide by our rules. I didn't want him to be my pet, I wanted him to be part of my family. It was the least I could do.

Even though I was afraid I would pass on all my unresolved fear, guilt, shame, and resentment to my children, I didn't have that fear with Yueng. I could love him as a mother, and he gave me complete unconditional love back. What more could a girl ask for?

The biggest gift my fur baby has given me is that I got to watch and have a hand in his growth and development. I got to be a parent; a real parent of something I should be responsible for, not parent someone who should have been responsible for me.

Every time, without me saying a single word, he raises his paw to ask to come on to the couch or our bed, or waits patiently for his supper, I am immediately the super proud mum at their child's recital, watching them perform a concerto and feeling like their child is the only prodigy in the room. Instead of cutting crusts off kids' sandwiches and packing schoolbags, every day I get the ritual of grabbing the leash, poop bags, and treats as I go out to explore the world with Yueng by my side.

I also love that he not only gives me something to parent, but Joe too. I get to see Joe in the role of a father, something I otherwise never would have. We get to parent something helpless, dependent, and vulnerable together. We put up with the explosions of fur and the chewed socks and scratched floorboards because he brings us more joy into our lives than we could ever have hoped for.

We get to have something external to ourselves that we worry about, laugh at, and coo over. We both gush every time he curls up into a croissant on the couch or lays on the floor with his back legs splayed out like he is sunbathing.

He is our baby, and we get to be a family.

* * *

One winter evening, early in the pandemic, I came upstairs to the living room from my study. It was dark and pouring outside. Joe and the puppy were already ensconced on the couch with a blanket and watching TV.

I had just finished work and was brain-dead and exhausted. I flopped down onto the couch and squirmed my way between them, placing my head on Joe's chest. Yueng grumpily moved to give me space and repositioned himself to put his chin on my foot, before promptly falling back asleep. Joe lay his arm across my back, and I snuggled in further, listening to his steady, slow heartbeat, and my head rose and fell in sync with his breathing. Yueng twitched and started sleep barking. I reached down and lay my hand gently on his back until he stopped.

It was peaceful, calm, and safe.

This is what it feels like to be happy! *This* is my turn!

CHAPTER 19

Gas Station Meat

———

I'm sure this surprised no one more than Joe himself, but since moving to Seattle, he has become a camper. Before we met, I think he'd been camping a total of twice in his life. Now, we try to go at least four to five times a summer, and he's even been once without me.

I used to go camping all the time when I was home in Melbourne. I did it with school and then in the Scouts and after that just with friends. I loved the connection with nature and the activities it provided, despite the hazards going bush in Australia posed.

That's one of the things I love about living in the Pacific Northwest: the easy access to amazing camping and incredible scenery without being constantly on the lookout for the vast array of venomous reptiles or biting insects.

We have a spot we like to go camping just south of Mount Rainier. There is a sweet campsite with a grove of old-growth trees and is right by the river. In the summertime for the past five or so years, Joe and I have gone down there with an assortment of friends to camp for long weekends.

There is something old-world magical about that place.

I don't know if it is the smell of the fresh earth or the river loaded with icy water from the glacial melt. It could also be the lowland forest of red alder, huge mature black cottonwood, and willow trees providing our camp shelter and character.

Whenever we go there, even if it is only for a couple of days, I feel rejuvenated.

It is the one of the few times Joe unplugs and we can sit together with no distraction of TV or the internet; just great conversations and laughs or quiet contemplation, with the sound of the rushing river, the birds chirping in the distance, and the dog running around the campsite through the scrub or kicking up dust behind us.

This particular camping trip was in the summer over Memorial Day weekend, so we got there early to nab the spot and stake out room for our friends.

When we arrived, we walked down to the river and unloaded our gear. I pulled out the camp chair and placed it facing the water. No one else was there yet. The sun slanted down through the trees, backlighting the leaves and the hovering bugs, before bouncing off the strongly flowing current. It was beautiful and serene.

After our long drive, Joe wanted to drop all the gear and head into town to get some dinner and firewood for the camp-fire that night. I wanted to stay put, but, as was my usual M.O., I didn't speak up. In my head, I knew what I wanted: for Joe to take the dog and give me a break from having to keep watch so I could do a session.

I had already taken an edible and wanted to sit back and soak up the atmosphere in meditative introspection while I had the late afternoon sunlight and the silence. I knew once everyone else arrived, that moment would be lost in the bustle of setting up camp and catching up.

But I didn't speak up. I didn't speak my truth. Instead, I put my desires on hold, loaded the dog back into the car, and went the couple of miles into town with Joe.

Joe wanted a burger, and by the time we got to the burger joint, he had asked me a few times already what I wanted to eat. I did my usual "acquiesce-and-stay-quiet". I didn't have the strength of conviction to ask for what I really wanted. "Whatever works, babe. Anything is fine," I eventually said noncommittally.

Inside my head, I was very clear. *No. I don't want a burger. That will mean waiting for, like, twenty to thirty minutes just for the food. I want whatever is fastest so we can get back to camp. I want gas station meat.*

Every time Joe and I go into the town gas station to get firewood or last-minute snacks and supplies, I am drawn by the inviting smell to their hot food counter and eye their assortment of fried foods. Wings, fries, Jojos (which I learned was the name for those huge potato wedges), and chicken strips, all glistening and tempting in their battered and crispy deliciousness.

I can't remember who came up with the term first, whether it was me or Joe, but since coining it, we forever refer to that collection of goodies as "gas station meat." So far, we had never been brave enough to try it, but that night, I couldn't resist the smell or the promised convenience.

"I want gas station meat," I finally spoke up when Joe asked again what I wanted to order as we pulled up to the restaurant. "Really? You want to chance that?" he asked, only half-joking. "Well, I don't. I'm getting a burger."

In the end, I got one too, as I still had to wait while he got his dinner and the daylight was already waning. We stopped at the gas station on the way back to camp to get the firewood, and I waited in the car. Joe came out with a fragrant steaming box, and I knew my real desires had been answered.

"You got me gas station meat!" I squealed with delight and laughter.

"Okay, so now you have this, you aren't having any burger. I'm giving it to the dog or saving it for later. Enjoy your food Russian roulette," Joe joked, handing me the box. As it turned out, the gas station meat was delicious, and Joe ended up eating as much of it as I did.

The insight that came with the meal, however, was more important to me than my full stomach. I realized in that moment that even with all the progress with my sessions and self-awareness, I still had issues knowing who I was and asking for what I truly wanted.

It would have been so much easier for me, and clearer for Joe, if I had just said from the outset, "No, thanks. I don't want to go into town. I want to sit here by the river and do a session. Can you please take the dog and bring me back some food when you're done?"

But I didn't say that. I said nothing, like I had been trained to do.

Growing up with my dad, I learned to doubt myself. I doubted every decision, every emotion, and every reaction. I couldn't think for myself and needed external validation for every move. I had him in the back of my brain for years—always deferring to him for how I should live my life.

Would Dad approve?

It was the first question I asked myself about any situation or life choice. And I only did it if the answer was *yes*.

* * *

When I was in high school, I wanted to be a writer.

I loved stories. I loved understanding character motivations. I loved plot twists I didn't see coming. I loved the rhythm of words and sentences and I always had snippets in my head.

I loved them because they were my escape. I dove into fantasy worlds and lived vicariously through the characters on the pages. I felt safe with the protagonist and awe for the heroes of the stories. I needed good mirror neurons to fire. I stayed away from horror and shied away from suspense. I needed romance and travel and humor and even science fiction; maybe a few light murder mysteries or adventure books for good measure.

I wanted so desperately to be creative, but I wasn't allowed. It wasn't something my father let me do. He needed me to be practical. I needed to have real, valuable, survival-level skills. I needed to have a trade so I could survive if shit went down. Being creative didn't help you survive when you were being hunted or starving in a ditch. Being practical did. Knowing how to use your hands, how to build or cook, mend tools, farm, or milk a cow—whatever it was you could use to leverage a way to exist.

Writing poems, telling stories or studying Shakespeare wasn't going to keep a roof over my head or food in my belly. I needed to be a secretary, or maybe get a job in a shop or a factory. That was it. That was my father's sum total of ambition for me.

When every other child's parent told their kids they could be anything and do anything if they just set their mind to it, my father was telling me, "You can do anything you want to do, as long as it's what I want you to do."

Fuuuuuuuuck! Not this again! How many ways was I going to find that this directive had stunted my growth?

I felt like I had no choice. I was trapped. I couldn't speak up for myself and I couldn't have a say in what I wanted my life to be. I had to do what he said. I had to do it his way. I had to be a good little girl and not think for myself.

Don't be who you really are. Be who I tell you to be. Don't be fully you. Be a reflection of me.

My inner spark spoke to me back when I was eighteen, just like it did when I was in the bottom of the pit. It told me this isn't what I'm meant to be or do. It's what made me push so hard to go to university. After a year of secretarial studies straight out of high school, it was clear it just wasn't for me. Instead, I got myself into university but to study science and computing, still choosing practical subjects to appease my father.

In my career, I ended up being a user experience (UX) designer because I kept trying to find the most practical way of being creative. But I'm not a designer. I'm not a network administrator. I'm not a business analyst or project manager or trainer, even though I've successfully been doing those things. It's not who I'm meant to be. In my heart, I'm a writer. Apart from journaling and that cycling column, I've not really let myself be one since puberty.

Being a writer was scary for me, because it implied I was a thought leader. Which then would require me to think. I didn't even want to know or listen to my own thoughts, so why would anyone else? What could I possibly offer?

Before doing the ayahuasca and healing sessions, I struggled to articulate who I was or to ask for what I wanted because I didn't know the real me. How could I, when I'd been constantly hiding parts of myself away?

But now I have direct access to those parts of me again, so I remember viscerally what it felt to be them at their age and in their circumstances. I have their words, their version of the world, at my fingertips. My writer's voice is my parts' voices all having a chance to be heard and ready to tell their story on the page, declaring what they want and need.

Now, thanks to plant medicine, the part of Michelle who loved to write is back. It got me out of my own way so I could let the thoughts and feelings come out onto the page. It provided the ideas swimming around my brain a conduit to escape.

Not only did it help me reassemble my parts and find my writer's voice, but the plant medicine also helped me realize I deserve to be heard and to ask for what I want.

* * *

Later that night, after we got back to camp with the firewood and the food, I told Joe, "Babe, I'm sorry. All these years I've been so unclear. No wonder you never knew what I wanted and accused me of constantly changing my mind. I could never identify or own what I really wanted in the first place, so how were you ever able to give it to me? I feel like I set you up to fail from the beginning."

Joe just looked at me. Again, this was not news to him. He had pointed out to me on more than one occasion that I said one thing and did another. He knew I didn't know my own mind.

Later that evening, sitting around the campfire with a drink and the dog on my lap, I asked myself, *What do I really want?*

The answer did not surprise me.

I want peace and calm. I want safety for me and all those I know and love. I want to feel special, adored, and loved. I want to be successful. I want all the things I was told I wasn't allowed to be: feminine, sexy and attractive, curious, passionate, playful, and loud. I want to be independent, able to think for myself and feel my emotions. I want to be proud of my body. Fuck, not just that, I want to be in my body. At all times. I want to breathe. I want out of my current job. I want to be a writer.

I want to LIVE!

It took a moment to let that sink in before I finally realized the last piece of the puzzle.

The only one stopping me from having all I want is *me*—not my father or my history.

I chose where I was in life right now. I chose the house I live in, the job I had, and my relationship with Joe; the fact I was in Seattle. All of that I chose, because I was never forced at any step of the way. I chose everything!

As soon as I realized it was all my choice, I realized I'm responsible for everything in my life. I may not have felt like it was when I was a kid, but I was then too—at least, how I reacted and felt about things and what I chose to do. It was exactly what Dr. Edith Eger talked about in her book, *The Choice*, as did Vicktor Frankl in his book, *Man's Search for Meaning*. I finally embodied the power of accountability and freedom.

Now I don't ask, "Would Dad approve?" I ask, "What do I want?"

It's still very much a work in progress, and I fail often, but I am getting better at listening to my heart. Now I have defrosted so many more parts, their voices are easier to hear and understand. I can do or be anything I can imagine. I can have joy and success and step out from being the victim.

Now I know, I want gas station meat.

CHAPTER 20

Oh, How I Appreciate You

———

I've been practicing looking at myself in the mirror these past few years and telling myself, "I love you, Shayla, Michelle, Mitch Malek."

The practice didn't come in the saying—it came in the believing.

Believing I could love myself was always the challenge. Believing I *deserved* to love myself, that I was *capable* of loving myself, or that I even *knew how* to love myself was what I needed to practice.

For far too long, the parts of me who were proud of myself, my intellect, my body, and my accomplishments spent too long numb and entombed in the deepest part of my ice prison. They were the parts of me who wore sexy dresses and felt good about myself. Those parts where I was slim and athletic, did my hair and makeup, and reveled in my femininity; when I took care of myself and stepped into my power. Those were the moments when I got the most negative feedback from Dad. They were the ones with the longest sentences, the ones that only got to come out of prison on short-term release and with a monitored ankle bracelet. They were repeat offenders and kept under the tightest lock and key.

As a result they were the parts I scorned the most and treated as the most dangerous.

I had no compassion for my younger self or why she locked those parts away. As Mitch, and for a lot of the time as Shayla, I was the first person who deserted Michelle. I spent my time putting myself down long after Dad's voice faded.

If I didn't even want or love myself, how could I expect anyone else to?

*   *   *

Sometime in the middle of 2020, Joe was at work and I was lying on the couch. I'd taken an edible and started to feel its effects. The house was quiet, and I was luxuriating in having it all to myself. Yueng was on the rug below me, gnawing on a bone.

My mind thought about the archway I'd seen in my ayahuasca trip and what I still needed to do to pass through it. I'd come a fair way, but I was still on this side of the finish line. "If you want to heal, just let go," I heard Mother Aya say again in my brain. "Just let all the pain go." But I couldn't.

I lay on the couch with my hands clasped tightly together, clutched to my chest. I let myself follow my body's lead and tried not to question what was happening. In my mind, one hand was mine and the other was Dad's. I didn't want to let him go. I hung on for dear life.

I imagined I was about four or five years old, when Dad was still my hero, big and strong, and I looked to him for protection.

Just let go, Michelle. Just let go. You will be okay. You will survive. I promise, I told myself as current-day Shayla.

But I couldn't let go. I was still frozen.

My attention shifted, and I felt a tightness in my chest. An urgency to move and scream. I sat up suddenly and swung my feet to the floor. I was a tightly wound spring with energy to release and nowhere to release it. I started bouncing my legs and stamping my feet. Yueng felt the shift in my mood and immediately came over to me.

I was restless. I got up to look for something to eat. I opened each cupboard, but nothing appealed because I wasn't really hungry.

I know what this is, I thought as I said *no* and went back to the couch. *I'm stuck. I'm anxious. It's in my body,* I realized. I moved my hands all over my body, looking for spots of tension. When I found one, I pressed hard with my thumb, holding it there until the tightness and pain eased, and my body responded with a huge, spontaneous intake of breath. I slowly moved all over from my head to my shoulders, pecs, groin, and legs, probing for points of pain to release. The weed helped me tune into myself with a level of focus I'm not normally able to achieve. With each deep breath, I unfurled my posture that much more and, with it, gained new perspectives and insights.

Okay. So, time for a new start. A new beginning, I continued thinking as current-day Shayla.

Again? Always again! I'm never able to keep at something consistently, my mind shot back.

Why?

Fuck knows. Discipline? Or lack thereof!

Is that it? Really, truly it? I doubt it. Fear, more like. Fear of Dad. Fear of failure. Fear of success.

Really? This shit again? And again and again! It can just fuck right off. Seriously. I mean it.

"Fuck off!" I yelled out loud to no one in particular and startled the dog.

How do I get beyond this? Move forward?

I don't know. I really don't know.

But if I did know?

I focused on what my body was telling me. I was tight in the shoulders and across my back. A hard kernel of shame and fear and hate.

Hate?

Yes. Hate. Self-hate. Self-doubt and shame. Fuck!

Why the self-hate? Why the shame?

I don't know.

Why can't I forgive myself like I forgive others? Forgive myself and move on? Let go?

I don't know.

But if you did know? What's your first thought? I probed deeper.

Because I don't truly believe I deserve it. I don't believe I am a good person. I let my father down. I betrayed his trust. He needed me. He needed me, and I let him down.

And then the realization hit me. I was so deeply attached to being the victim. I couldn't, or wouldn't, let myself imagine a life where I had regained my power and full autonomy.

I don't know how to live my life without him, for good or for bad, directing me from the shadows. I don't know how to stand on my own two feet and think for myself.

At that thought, I wanted to scream. And scream. And scream. Like I do sometimes in the car. The frustration was palpable. I turned and screamed into a pillow. I let the pain out, my frustration and sadness and shame, until my throat was raw and my voice scratchy and feeble.

Once I was spent, I lay back down on the couch and realized I was still clasping my hands tightly together.

Let go, Michelle, I said gently to myself. *I promise I won't let you fall. You've got this,* I tried again talking to that frozen part of me. I closed my eyes and imagined my younger self walking hand-in-hand with my father. I was five and seven and ten and twenty-two years old all at the same time.

"Dad, I've got this. I'm going to let go now," I said, gently but firmly, as I turned to him in my mind's eye.

"Okay, love," he responded after a pause, giving my hand one last squeeze as we disengaged and then walked contentedly next to each other for a little bit longer.

I opened my eyes and saw that my hands were unclasped, and I sat up and smiled. Then I got up from the couch and stood there, swaying slightly from side to side before I went and turned on some music and danced around the house.

* * *

Given the success I had with my weed sessions, I decided to give mushrooms another go. I stopped eating at seven the night before and took them first thing in the morning. I was delighted to find I didn't have nausea this time, but even the small dose I took hit me like a tornado.

My perception of reality was blown away. I saw pretty colors and patterns, the same as before, but this time I had more clarity of mind and purpose. I repeated my intention: *I want to heal*—the same as when I met Mother Aya. I went down to my study and lay on the floor, letting the sensations wash over me and the emotions emerge.

Suddenly, without any provocation, I started crying. I imagined I was lying between Mum and Dad, holding their hands.

I turned to face my father.

"Dad, I forgive you," I said, tears clogging my throat.

From all those years of Co-counseling, I learned to distinguish between a person and their patterns of behavior. It's never black or white, good or evil. I learned to recognize that my father was not a bad person, but that he did bad things. I don't excuse or condone his behavior, but I have learned to forgive the scared, sad, hurt little boy hiding inside the man my father became.

I knew his father, my grandfather, was not a model of a kind, gentle man. As a child even before the war, Dad was beaten, yelled at, treated as a burden, and something to be used to gain pity when they were out begging.

"Now I see you. I see your pain and suffering and trauma," I said to him. "I wish nothing more than for you to be alive so I could say I'm sorry for what you went through. I know I never said it to you when I had the chance. I was never able to just sit and tell you I loved you, because I was always too scared.

"I understand where you were at. I understand you were so young and all alone through some of the worst trauma a person can endure. I understand later how difficult it must have been for you, trying to raise a family and working as hard as you did. You were slightly younger than I am now when you had your third child. I know how exhausted I am at this age, and I'm only responsible for myself and the dog! "I get how hard it is to give up everything you know and love to move to the other side of the world. I see how you existed on so few parts of yourself. I get that you were frozen. I get you needed help. I understand you were scared, sad, lonely, and frustrated too. You had every right to be angry at the world."

I saw my dad in that moment like I would see one of my friends; one of my peers. Not the big, scary, looming adult who was the authority in my life. From that sense of perspective, I saw his flaws and his good attributes.

I remembered how concerned he was whenever any of us were sick and how well he looked after our dogs and even the fish. He was an honest man and worked so hard to provide for us. I remembered how he tried to take part in local politics to help those less fortunate. I could now focus on remembering the times when he was warm and playful.

I remembered fondly being a little kid and playing on his knee. I used to smush his face, and he would let me. He would put me on his feet and dance me across the room. He always tried to be there for me when I needed him.

I imagined my father turning to me and saying, "Thank you, Misha. I'm so very sorry for what I did. I didn't mean to hurt you. I know I had a short fuse. I wanted to keep you close. I wanted someone to love me, someone who I wouldn't lose. I'm so proud of you. So proud of how you've turned out. You are a credit to the family and to yourself. I wish you every success in life." As he said it, he looked genuinely happy, like the time he said at my twenty-first birthday, overcome with emotion, "I love you."

At those words, I sobbed harder, but the heaviness in my heart lifted. I swallowed and cleared my throat.

Then I turned to the other side to face my mother. "Mum," I said to her. "I love you so much. I'm sorry I never got to have the kind of relationship with you I truly wanted. I know you tried your hardest and honestly did the best you could. I know you were scared too. I was so busy resenting you for not being there when I needed you as a kid that I held back from you as an adult and wasted so much time. You were always fair and kind, trying to express your love through books or food, even through the hardest times. You were always there for me as an adult whenever I needed you, in whatever way you could."

Mum looked at me and smiled. "Michelle, you know I

love you. I always have. I'm sorry you feel I wasn't there for you when you needed me the most, or that I didn't want you. If I had my time over, I'd do it differently. You are strong, and you are smart, and you are going to do just fine."

I lay back down and let the tears come unchecked. I cried and sobbed and wailed. I missed them both so much. I let the tears wash away all my grief, anger, resentment, and regrets. I saw them as people. I saw them as flawed and human. I felt their pain and their sorrow as deeply as I felt mine.

Through all the work I have done, I have come to peace with what happened and am moving on. It doesn't serve me or anyone else in my life to hang on to the shame or blame I had around my childhood. In that session, I finally forgave myself and them. I recognized that, like them, I also tried to do the best I could under the circumstances.

They weren't perfect, and neither am I.

* * *

A few weeks ago, Joe and I had some friends over to watch my newest favorite entertainment, sumo wrestling. I snuggled on the couch with Joe in his usual spot to the left of me, and to my right was my close friend, Britt. Our Burner friends, Emily and Alex, Justin and Kyla, and Elizabeth and her dog, Alibi, were sprawled out on the floor on cushions and camp chairs.

I got up from my cozy spot on the couch to go to the loo. When I finished, I went to wash my hands and caught sight of my reflection in the mirror.

My immediate thought was, *Wow, Shay. I love your hair!*

Since the beginning of the pandemic, I have tried to take better care of myself and put my love for myself into everyday practice, starting with trying to defrizz my hair. I tried all sorts of hair products and treatments, and finally it looked like something was working.

My hair was looking shiny and smooth, and that was without any products. I was immediately so proud of myself that I took some selfies to capture the moment and for comparison purposes.

I clearly didn't realize they were waiting for me to start the show again, because when I finally came out of the bathroom, they were all looking at me.

Joe laughed and said, "Yeah, she's been in there modeling. Taking photos and shit. I always know when she does that because she takes forever and comes out looking hot!"

Everyone laughed, and I immediately started to explain it was to record my hair progress, not because I was full of myself, but I stopped.

No one was getting me in trouble because I spent time admiring myself and being proud of the progress I'd made with my hair. No one, not even Joe, was saying I was vain or bad or shameful because I'd been taking selfies. They all laughed in a loving, knowing way, and someone (I think it was Emily or maybe Britt) even agreed with Joe's assessment of my hotness.

They accepted me being me. They *loved* me being me.

But that wasn't important. *I* loved me being me. In the back of my mind, I felt my parents being proud of me too.

I love you, Shayla, Michelle, Mitch Malek, I silently affirmed as I got back onto the couch and turned my attention back to the TV.

CHAPTER 21

Agents of Change

———

"I've been thinking a lot about death lately," I said out of the blue, turning to face Joe early one Saturday morning not too long ago. It was the middle of November, and our bedroom was chilly. We were in bed to keep warm, tangled up together under the covers with Yueng draped over Joe's legs.

"Oh?" He laughed nervously. "Um, that's nice... and not even the littlest bit creepy!" he said, quickly pulling away from me and scrambling to the other side of the bed in mock fear of his life.

"And not even in a pandemic, riots, overthrowing the Capitol or BLM kind of way," I continued, trying to keep a straight face at his reaction. Although, let's be real, that's never far from my mind.

"No. It's more like I've been thinking about death as a catalyst for growth and as an agent of change," I declared, quite proud of myself as I tried to snuggle closer to him. But he wasn't buying it and squirmed out of my reach. He looked at me warily, as if at any minute, like a magician pulling a rabbit out of a hat, I would suddenly be brandishing a machete or gun in my hand. I laughed and stopped teasing him.

I gave up trying to cuddle with Joe and moved instead to give my affection to the dog, who, disturbed by Joe's sudden movement, was now nestled up beside me. His velvety muzzle rested heavily on my shin, using it as a pillow. Yueng looked quizzically at me as I rearranged myself, so I spooned around him and absent-mindedly stroked the soft fur behind his ears. I didn't have any desire that morning in bed, comfortable, cozy, and in my happy place, to elaborate to Joe just how much death still was, and always had been, on my mind. Dad always impressed upon me, through words and actions, how fleeting life was, and that was even before I lost Mum. Even now, after all my healing efforts and growth, I was still somewhat petrified that death would take away those I love before I even have a chance to say goodbye.

I sighed at that thought, instinctively reached out with my foot to connect with Joe, and hugged Yueng tightly, but it wasn't that kind of death I was thinking about.

"They had to die," I said after a while, my voice deadpan.

"What?" Joe asked sharply. "Who had to die?"

"My limiting beliefs and victim mentality. Obviously."

"Oh, and my ego," I added as an afterthought. "I couldn't have had the inner changes I did if they hadn't all died."

"Did they die from ninja stars or throwing knives? Maybe ray guns or dismemberment?" Joe asked hopefully. "A stiletto through the eye?"

"Ew, no. None of those gruesome movie deaths," I said, taking the bait. "It was a dignified, asleep in bed, surrounded-by-your-loved-ones-at-ninety kind of death."

I wanted to create an obituary in my mind: a wall of honor and reverence to those parts of me that, as Michelle and Mitch and later as Shayla, I created to guard me in order to survive. I thought about how allowing those parts of me to die had provided the space and means for other, more beneficial parts of me to live and thrive. I had recycled the detritus of my past pain to feed and nurture my new self. I was mycelium breaking down the decaying remains of the forest floor, redistributing the nutrients amongst its network as building blocks for new life.

Most importantly, I finally let my emotional tether to my dad of guilt, shame, and fear wither and die. It died of neglect and malnutrition. Every time I did a session, stood a little taller with self-pride, had a new healthy insight, did some creative writing, or basically followed my ayahuasca path of lights, I starved the darkness feeding that psychosomatic parasite.

Now, at last, after all that death and change, I finally feel like I know who I am. I am no longer a victim. I am a survivor. I am not a survivor of any war, rape, or abduction, but I am a survivor of emotional abuse and trauma. My father was also a survivor. He was resourceful and courageous and resilient, but he was also broken and hurt, angry and sad, needy and controlling, and at times, violent and abusive. That also makes me a survivor of a survivor.

But that's not all I am. I, like everyone else, am so much more than the single part of my identity I choose to wear at any one moment in time; the parts I play on high rotation because they are familiar, easy, and comfortable. Daughter, sister, friend, lover—all roles I play and only a fraction of my true self. When I flip over the tape to the B side, I am also a dancer, writer, cyclist, photographer, explorer, dog mom, or podcaster.

*   *   *

When I think back, I can't help but see with gratitude the perfect clusterfuck of events that conspired to throw me so far off track of my emotional through line that I couldn't have planned it better if I tried.

The effects of the ayahuasca changing my life rippled from the moment of ingestion up and down my timeline, affecting every decision that led me to the next step of my life. I truly believe I could not have had the incredible healing I've had without the right things first falling into place.

I had to meet Joe, fall in love, move to Seattle, do weed and then psychedelics so I would eventually be comfortable enough to drink ayahuasca. I followed each of the lights Mother Aya left me to guide my way. The trail led me back to the finish line. I've got that archway firmly in my sights. I'm not quite there yet, but I'm closer than I've ever been.

It was like the universe, or my spirit, that spark inside me, pulled every trick in the book to get me into an emotional pressure cooker situation so I would be forced to dig deep into my own grit and resourcefulness to learn how to finally heal and not just survive.

I also knew it was going to be slow going. I'm constantly finding more parts to release and reintegrate. Despite that, I can see progress. My mood is now more often positive than negative. I am doing creative things and prioritizing myself and my needs.

I'm still working on it every day, and this book has catapulted that growth exponentially. Just sitting down to write these words has been the most incredible personal challenge I have ever accepted and, at the same time, the greatest gift of insight I've ever been given.

I know I've told myself before that I want to heal, and I'm going to do better, and somehow I always ended up self-sabotaging. This time feels different. I feel lighter in my heart since I started doing the plant medicine. Each of those lanterns the ayahuasca laid as a trail for me to follow out of my pit of depression is still burning brightly inside my chest. They are making me glow from the inside in a swirling array of fluorescent, fractalizing patterns, repeating and repeating in on themselves.

Inside the ice prison is now a disco. Lasers and lights of multiple shapes and colors refract and bounce off every surface like an exploded glitter bomb. My heart is luminescent and soaring.

I'm also lighter because each of those ice cells are empty. I'm not carrying around the weight in my chest that pinned me to the bottom of the pit; the weight of my frozen heart. Now the pit has almost gone, almost erased from sight. But when I look closely at my heart, I can still see the scars. They're puckered and dried, and the wounds haven't completely disappeared, they are still there as reminders.

As much as the world keeps trying to drag me down with its doom scrolling and messages of hate and fear, I am not going to let myself get mired in the cesspools of negativity. Almost every day I remind myself to choose to take a different path than the one anxiety has taken me down before. Whenever I feel scared or overwhelmed, I ask myself, *Shayla, right here, in this moment, right now, are any of those bad things happening to you or the people you love? The things you are so frightened of?* Invariably the answer is always *no,* so I let out the breath I was holding. Then I look around and see the things I'm grateful for—my home, Joe, the dog, friends, and family—and remember that being scared all the time is not living and I can choose to chill the fuck out instead.

*   *   *

"Remember how hard it was for me?" I said to Joe, returning to our conversation. "When I first arrived in Seattle, I was so uptight, so passive aggressive, so easily upset and annoyed, and we fought over every little thing?" I continued.

I had his attention now.

"Yes. I remember. You were a bitch," he teased.

"I was. And you were an asshole," I shot back just as quickly. "We've both grown a lot since then," I acknowledged, and he nodded.

There was no malice in either of our words. We both recognized how challenging those times were. We both knew that back then, even though we loved each other 100 percent, to be truthful, most of the time we only really liked each other about half that, sometimes even less. I was scared, I was sad, and I was half-dead inside. It was an understatement to say I wasn't fun to be around.

"I couldn't have paid for more effective therapy," I joked, acknowledging the pain of those times but also the rewards.

Joe just grunted a distracted reply, his attention back on his phone. This wasn't news to him. Not only had he heard this before, he'd lived it with me.

"It only took about eight or so years."

"For what?" he asked, confused, trying to pick up the thread of our conversation from a few minutes earlier.

"For me to change. To learn how to let myself fully live," I replied. "To finally grieve and let go. To restore all those lost parts of myself and come out of the freeze. I couldn't have done it without you and the plant medicine. And the puppy, of course!" I quickly added, giving Yueng a scratch behind the ears. "Thank you," I said, acknowledging his part in that growth, reaching over to kiss him and forcing him to pay attention to me rather than to his phone. "I know it has been one hell of a ride. I've still got a long way to go, but I feel like I've come a long way since then too."

I could tell he was going to answer with a long reply but thought better of it.

"Yes. You have," he agreed and went back scrolling Twitter.

I lay back on the pillow and allowed my thoughts to turn to appreciation of the parts of me I had revived. I stretched and breathed in and luxuriated in the feeling of fresh clean air filling my lungs. The feeling of peace, gratitude, and contentment now filled the center of me instead of the fear and sadness that never filled the void.

I loved that I could now tune into my body and actually feel it from the inside. I connected with my emotions and where in my heart they resided. I loved, too, that I now appreciate and look after my outside. I take more care of my skin and hair and exercise again.

"Of course you did. You're a 'doer,'" my physical therapist, Kelly, casually proclaimed after I told her all the times I completed my homework exercises.

A "'doer." 'Yes, I am. I had forgotten that part of me; the one where I looked forward to doing, rather than just sitting back and being jealous of what others had done. I was no longer *move, distract, do*-ing. Now I was *dream, plan, do*-ing, just like Mother Aya had promised.

I loved that I had discovered what I really wanted and who I really was. I had reinvigorated my drive and ability to challenge myself and push through until I accomplished what I desired. I loved even more that, once again, I had the energy for living, exploring, and finding things that made me thrive. I was now a full opacity version of me. All my layers turned back up to full intensity. I had reintegrated Misha, Michelle, and Mitch into Shayla and welcomed them back into me. I listened as the adult with love and patience to their tales of pain, then did the work it took to heal them. For the first time ever, I was so proud of myself, and they were too.

"Where are you going? It's barely 7:30!" Joe asked in surprise as I suddenly sat bolt upright beside him, disturbing him and the dog with my urgent, energetic display.

"I've got writing to do!" I said and sprung out of bed, landing squarely on my feet, ready to start my day.

ACKNOWLEDGMENTS

———

I could fill an entire book on its own with the names of people I need to thank in my life, all those people who showed me kindness, love, support, or affection. There are simply too many to name individually, and I don't want to leave anyone out, as you have all contributed to my well-being over the years. Please know when I mention a group of people, I mean all those folks who were part of that group or community. You know who you are, and I know who you are.

There are a couple of people, however, I am going to specifically call out.

First to my sister Cherie.

I could not have survived my childhood without her. Literally.

Even though I had my mum's family of aunts, uncles and cousins who always showed us love and kindness, she was right there in the trenches with me and has so many of the same battle scars. I love her more than I can say. She stayed when she should have gone. She stayed to look out for me and, in many ways, was a buffer between me and Dad. She gave me a safe refuge when she finally moved out and then gave me courage to do the same. She was the trailblazer paving the way.

Thank you, Cherie, for all you have done. I know staying took its toll on you, and I am more grateful than you can know.

* * *

Every time I say I love you to Joe or the dog, or I tell them how cute they are, or how happy I am they are with me, I'm in the present. I savor that moment of peace and calm and the simple pleasures of love and connection.

I feel safe in that moment and feel the gratitude in my body when I say those things. Those verbal tokens of appreciation come from a place of wholeheartedness, and whole-soul-ness, that I want to live in forever.

It is because of my relationship with Joe I was able to glimpse that promised land within me. He was always right there beside me in the emotional mosh pit. He became, as Glennon Doyle calls it in her book, *Untamed*, my Touch Tree. He was who I always came back to. Even from the bottom of my pit, he was my North Star I saw in the sky overhead; my home base. We bounced off each other, jouncing around in our little cocooned life, just the two of us, both separated geographically from family, old friends, and old lives. We mostly revolved around each other even before the pandemic, and during it even more so. It was because of those constant revolutions inside the gem tumbler of a relationship that I learned about myself; so I even had something to put down on these pages.

Joe was my mirror; my antagonist too. At least, I made him out to be. I dumped onto him all the unprocessed and raw responses I had shored up after a lifetime of living as me. All my learned patterns of behavior were projected onto him along with my romantic notion of who I wanted him to be.

Happily, we came out of it a little battle scarred but stronger for the go-round. Eventually we had had so many go-rounds that our hard edges were knocked off and smoothed out, so we fit together more seamlessly.

I want to tell him and I want him to know:

Joe, my heart swells so much when I think of you. I can't even begin to describe how thankful I am to you for sticking it out with me. You were by my side 100 percent of the time. You never left me. You were sage and smart, spot-on and incredibly sassy at times. You didn't buy into my bullshit. You called me out on my games. There was no hiding from you.

I needed a rock, and you were solid. I owe you a debt of thanks that cannot be repaid. Your soul clearly made an agreement with mine to help me heal, and I hope I've helped you too. You were perfectly all the things I needed you to be so I could see what held me back and kept me down. You helped me set myself free.

Thank you. Thank you. Thank you.

Thank you also to Joe's family (and friends), who have been nothing but warm, welcoming, gracious, and kind. I felt accepted and part of the family from the moment he introduced me.

*   *   *

I also want to sincerely thank every single person I call family and every friend I've ever made, from school, university, Confest, CCI, work, Scouts, house sharing, cycling, camping, or any other way. You are important to me. Every one of you helped me along the way.

It's not just the people I grew up with back home as Michelle and later as Mitch and Shayla—it's also the people I met and lived with on my travels and those in Seattle I've gotten to know over the years: the crew from our first ever apartment building, the people from work, the ones we already knew before we got here from the internet, and all the Burners I've met.

To the people who invited us to parties, had us over for cookouts and to watch the fireworks; to those who hosted us for Thanksgiving or Friday night dinners and Christmas lunches, Halloween parties and sitting around eating pizza or watching the Super Bowl; the people who went camping with us, the friends who met up with me so I could walk the dog or go for dinner and a movie. I am so grateful to you all. You helped me feel connected when I was at my most untethered. I'm so appreciative of connections even as small and tenuous as they may have seemed; chats with my massage or physical therapist or chiropractor; casual conversations in the work kitchen over a coffee; teams I joined and managers who were there for me. It meant so much to me. Without it, I felt exposed, lost, and lonely.

Without the love at home from Joe and the puppy, my friends at work, and the other friends I've made along the way, I couldn't have made it this far.

Thank you!

A special note goes out to all the people who barely knew me, Joe included, but helped me celebrate my forty-third birthday. I'd been in Seattle about seven months, and it was my first birthday since my mum had died. I was away from my family and old friends. I was dying inside.

Everyone made an effort. Joe got me presents and made a fuss. We went bowling with friends and had drinks and a great time. Alana and Jess from work took me out for lunch, drinks, and karaoke at the Rock Box.

It was the best birthday present I could have received.

I was going to be okay. I had people who cared. I wasn't alone.

Thank you! It meant more to me than any of you could have known.

* * *

For those who directly helped me write this book, I want to thank Katie Duke, who first introduced me to Jeff Leisawitz's workshop on creativity in 2019. It was Jeff who first encouraged me to write and gave me positive feedback on the small sample he saw. It gave me the hope that I did have the skills to write my father's book. Then, Katie told me about the Book Creator course run by Professor Koester through Georgetown University. The people in that course and everyone at New Degree Press gave me the structure, accountability, insane deadlines, and community that supported me enough to sit down and write my story.

Thank you especially to my first-ever developmental editor, Regina Stribling. She not only gave me instructive and insightful feedback on my writing but was crucial in quelling my first-time writer nerves. I wouldn't have finished my first draft without her. In addition, I want to thank all my beta readers, in particular, Cherie King, Dawn Nicholson, Ann Dimatteo, Jess Gray, Julie Schwager, Ilka Tiedemann, and Kayte Ashton. Thank you for the helpful, timely, and useful feedback when I needed it most. And, of course, Joe, who sat and listened through every iteration.

And last but certainly not least is all the people who generously contributed to my book launch campaign. Your support and blind faith in my sight-unseen work means the absolute world to me. It helped me feel like I wasn't alone on this creative journey.

Thank you!

Alana Kelton
Alexander Talsma
Alison Sondhi
Angela Cimadon
Anja Blom
Ann A. Jarvis
Ann Dimatteo
Anna Carew
Anna Spiteri
Anne Buchalski
Bec Fradkin
Brittany Burch
Carly Rappaport
Catherine Koetz
Cherie King
Daniel Jeffery
Daniel Kinal
Daniel Konigsberg
David Hobbs
Dawn Nicholson
Deb Marven
Denise McFadden
Donna Freeman
Elizabeth Roots
Emily Dobbins
Eric Koester
Gregory Mackenzie
Heather Petersen
Heather Yaeger
Ilka Tiedemann
Jacob Lemberg

James Lundie
Jason Tranchida
Jeffrey Leisawitz
Jenny Hanrahan
Jeremy Samuel
Jimi Lou Steambarge
Jocelyn Eillis
Joe Norris
Jonathan Cline
Joseph Graziano
Judy Hartling
Judy Kaminsky-Leitch
Julie Schwager
Jyrl Ann James
Karen Bird
Kathryn Bass
Kathryn Bergmann
Katie Duke
Kelly Johnson
Kelly Owens
Keridwyn Deller
Kristian Alexander
Kyla Drushka
Lance Alder
Lauren Bartleson
Leigh Hughes
Lesley Jones
Lois Calhoun
Marie Bird
Marissa Emmons
Marvin Campbell

Mary Klimek
Megan DeAtley
Melanie Nerenberg
Melissa Way
Michael Root
Miriam Hain
Nicole Goodman
Olivia Norris
Patricia Wreford-Brown
Phillip Radtke
Rebecca Jones
Robin Counts
Samantha Wood

Sarah Giles
Shelley Reed
Sonia Strong
Staci Civins
Sue Mandaville
Sumit Basu
Suzette Goldwasser
Tim Pritchard
Tommy Barnes
Toni Hackett
Tony Bohn
Yvonne Norris

CONTACT THE AUTHOR

Thank you for reading my story, and if you want to contact me, you can find me on Instagram **@shaylamalek** or on Facebook **@ShaylaMalekWriter** or through my website https://www.shaylamalek.com/contact

I've listed some resources on my website shaylamalek.com about psychedelic-assisted therapy and is also where I'll post photos and updates to continue the story.

APPENDIX

AUTHOR'S NOTE

Hope for Depression Research Foundation. "Depression Fact Sheet." 2021. https://www.hopefordepression.org/depression-facts.

Miller, Cody. Seattle City Council Votes in Favor of Decriminalizing Psychedelic Drugs. Updated. 11.08 AM PDT October 7, 2021. https://www.king5.com/article/news/local/seattle/seattle-city-council-favor-decriminalize-psychedelic-drugs.

CHAPTER 6: SO, HOW DO YOU FEEL?

Co-Counseling International–USA. "What is Co-Counseling?" Accessed June 6, 2022. https://www.cci-usa.org/what_is.php.

Brown, Brené. *The Power of Vulnerability: Teachings on Authenticity, Connection, and Courage.* Read by the author. Louisville: Sounds True, 2013. Audible audio.

Brown, Brené. *Atlas of the Heart: Mapping Meaningful Connection and the Language of Human Experience.* Read by the author. United States: Penguin Random House Audio Publishing Group, 2022.

Confest. "What is Confest?" Accessed June 6, 2022. https://confest.org.au/index.php/about/what-is-confest.

Department of Health, State Government of Victoria, Australia. "Bowen therapy." Accessed June 6, 2022. https://www.betterhealth.vic.gov.au/health/conditionsandtreatments/bowen-therapy.

Healthline Media a Red Ventures Company. "Is Rebirthing Therapy Safe and Effective?" Accessed June 6, 2022, https://www.healthline.com/health/rebirthing.

Hoffman Institute Foundation. "What is the Hoffman Process?" Accessed June 6, 2022. https://www.hoffmaninstitute.org/the-process.

Rolf Institute* of Structural Integration dba Dr. Ida Rolf Institute. "Home page." Accessed June 6, 2022, https://rolf.org.

The Tapping Solution Foundation. "What Is Tapping and How Does It Work?" Accessed June 6, 2022, https://www.tappingsolutionfoundation.org/howdoesitwork.

University of Pittsburgh Schools of the Health Sciences (UPMC). Life-Changing Medicine. "Craniosacral therapy." 2022. https://www.upmc.com/services/integrative-medicine/services/craniosacral-therapy.

CHAPTER 7: FUCK CANCER

The Hitchhiker's Guide to the Galaxy radio series. Originally broadcast in 1978, by BBC Radio 4, https://www.bbc.co.uk/comedy/hitchhikersguide/index.shtml.

CHAPTER 9: PORTION CONTROL

Morin, Roc. "Prescribing Mushrooms for Anxiety." April 22, 2014. The Atlantic. https://www.theatlantic.com/health/archive/2014/04/chemo-for-the-spirit-lsd-helps-cancer-patients-cope-with-death/360625/

Michael Pollan, How to Change Your Mind: What the New Science of Psychedelics Teaches Us About Consciousness, Dying, Addiction, Depression, and Transcendence. Narrated by the author. United Kingdom, Penguin Publishing Group, 2019.

CHAPTER 10: GOING INTO THE FREEZE

Dr. Aimie Apigian. Trauma Healing Accelerated Blog. "The Shocking Impact of Chronic Stress & Trauma on Your Genetics." Accessed January 24, 2022. https://draimie.com/the-shocking-impact-of-chronic-stress-trauma-on-your-genetics.

Health & Trauma Coach Dr. Aimie Apigian "Your 21 Day Journey to Consistent Calm Aliveness", Accessed January 24, 2022. https://traumahealingaccelerated.mykajabi.com/21-day-journey-to-calm-aliveness.

CHAPTER 12: AYA-WHAT-A?

MAPS (Multidisciplinary Association for Psychedelic Studies). "Our Mission." Accessed June 6, 2022, https://maps.org/about-maps/mission.

"The Joe Rogan Experience." Joe Rogan. *#782–Rick Doblin*, recorded April 7, 2016, no longer available. https://www.jrepodcast.com/episode/joe-rogan-experience-782-rick-doblin.

CHAPTER 15: 2020

Australia's Defining Moments Digital Classroom Website. "Our Vote = Our Future." Accessed June 13, 2022. https://digital-classroom.nma.gov.au/defining-moments/indigenous-australians-granted-right-vote.

BBC. "Two teenagers shot in Seattle's Chop autonomous zone." *BBC.com*, June 30, 2020. https://www.bbc.com/news/world-us-canada-53224445.

Guarino, Ben. "Man Who Allegedly Drove Car into Seattle Demonstration, Killing Protester, Charged with Homicide." *The Washington Post*. July 8, 2020. https://www.washingtonpost.com/nation/2020/07/08/seattle-protest-car-homicide.

Parliament of Australia. "2019-20 Australian Bushfires—Frequently Asked Questions: A Quick Guide." Published 12 March 2020, by Lisa Richards, Nigel Brew, Lizzie Smith. https://www.aph.gov.au/About_Parliament/Parliamentary_Departments/ Parliamentary_Library/pubs/rp/rp1920/Quick_Guides/AustralianBushfires.

The National Museum of Australia. "White Australia Policy." Updated: 31 August 2021. https://www.nma.gov.au/defining-moments/resources/white-australia-policy.

Watson, Joey. "A Brief History of Nazism in Australia." *ABC News*. Posted 16 Jan. 2019. https://www.abc.net.au/news/2019-01-17/a-history-of-nazis-and-the-far-right-in-australia/10713514.

CHAPTER 16: SESSION WORK

Keremedchiev, Simeon. "Psychedelics: Effects on the Human Brain and Physiology." Filmed November 19, 2016, TEDx Varna, Bulgaria. https://www.ted.com/tedx/events/21282.

CHAPTER 17: BE SEEN, BE HEARD

HBO TV series *Watchmen*, aired October 20-Dec 15, 2019. https://www.hbo.com/watchmen.

"The We Watch Podcast." Shayla Malek and Joe Norris. *A conversation on racism, Part 1*. Posted June 3, 2020. https://podcasts.apple.com/us/podcast/the-we-watch-podcast/id1483887699?i=1000476684882.

CHAPTER 19: GAS STATION MEAT

Dr. Edith Eva Eger. *The Choice: Embrace the Possible*. Narrated by Tovah Feldshuh

Simon & Schuster Audio, 2017.

Viktor E. Frankl, *Man's Search for Meaning*. Narrated by Simon Vance. Blackstone Audio, Inc. 2004.

ACKNOWLEDGMENTS

Doyle, Glennon. *Untamed*. Read by the author. Random House Audio, 2020.

Made in the USA
Monee, IL
31 March 2023

30618230R00128